THE BABYSITTER BOOK

John Cunningham trained as an actor at the Royal Academy of Dramatic Art and has since performed in repertory theatre all over Britain as well as on TV. Between roles he works with children's theatre groups and also minds children of all ages and backgrounds, including the handicapped.

Jennifer Curry originally trained as a teacher but has been a professional journalist for the past fifteen years. She is the author of twelve books covering school, children's and advice subjects and has written several plays, including three for children. She has two grown sons of her own.

THE BABYSITTER BOOK

HOW TO SOLVE ALL YOUR CHILDMINDING PROBLEMS

JOHN CUNNINGHAM
AND JENNIFER CURRY

Hamlyn Paperbacks

THE BABYSITTER BOOK
ISBN 0 600 20341 7

First published in Great Britain 1981
by Hamlyn Paperbacks
Copyright © 1981 by John Cunningham and
Jennifer Curry

Hamlyn Paperbacks are published by
The Hamlyn Publishing Group Ltd,
Astronaut House,
Feltham,
Middlesex, England

(Paperback Division: Hamlyn Paperbacks,
Banda House, Cambridge Grove,
Hammersmith, London W6 0LE)

This book is dedicated to all children, especially Kirsty, Adam, Lucy, Bif, Andy, Helen, Polly, David, Georgina, Rachel, Graeme, Ian, Nick, Stephen, Amanda, Douglas, Kenneth, Trudy, Dominic, Blair, Sharon, Ann, Evelyn, Mark, Masha, Sam. . .

Printed and bound in Great Britain by
Cox & Wyman Ltd, Reading

Note to the Reader

We are well aware that many of those involved in the world of babysitting and child care are male. Nevertheless, as a general rule to avoid confusion we have chosen to use the female pronoun throughout the book – both for the children and their minders.

J.C. and J.C.

The authors wish to thank the many organizations which gave their help and advice so willingly as well as those individuals who gave personal encouragement, especially Peter Tilbury and Caroline Boucher.

CONTENTS

INTRODUCTION

Babysitters have become an essential part of our way of life. And by babysitters we mean not only those people prepared to sit in with the children for a few hours so that their parents can have an evening out, but also the full range of professional child-carers, from the childminder to the au pair, from the local authority day nursery to the children's holiday playscheme.

It is a fact that today more mothers go out to work than in any peace-time period, but that nevertheless only a third of the women wanting day care for their children are actually able to find it. And it is reckoned that over half a million school-age children are left to fend for themselves for at least part of the day outside school hours. This leads us to the double conclusion that

★ more mothers would take jobs if their family commitments did not prevent them, and

★ many mothers who do have jobs are not finding satisfactory provision for their children while they are at work.

While researching this book we talked to hundreds of parents, fathers as well as mothers, and found that their urgent desire for good child care was based not on any lack of love for their families, a 'greedy' effort to achieve a more affluent way of life, or a selfish determination to pursue their own ambitions and careers regardless of their children's well-being. It was usually the result of a genuine and desperate *need*.

This need varies in its nature. It may be that a family can only survive financially if there are two earning adults in the household. In 1980 a report published by the Study Commission on the family revealed that *millions* of families relied upon the wife's income to keep them above the social security benefits net. Similarly, the majority of single parents – and in 1980 there were 920,000 of them in Britain – found that they must bring home a pay-packet if they were to provide their children with a tolerable standard of living. Some women possess special skills, talents or educational achievements that

9

the nation needs to draw on as part of its work-force if it is to prosper.

There is also an emotional and psychological need to work outside the home; not everyone can find total satisfaction in domesticity. Doctors are well aware that many women isolated in their houses with their children all day run the risk of depressive illness, of dependence on drink or tranquillizing drugs, or of psychosomatic illnesses or phobias. And, if their isolation is not relieved, it sometimes leads to child-battering, to marital breakdown . . . even to suicide.

The aim of this book is three-fold. It attempts to:
★ outline all the various babysitting and child-care facilities available so that parents know what to look for and how to find the best solution for their particular problem;
★ help parents create their own self-help patterns of child care when those provided for them are inadequate; and
★ advise them about the most efficient methods of persuading government, local authorities and employers to provide more and better facilities for their children.

It is not our intention to encourage parents to neglect their children. On the contrary, we hope that good child-care facilities will allow parents to return to their children refreshed, relaxed and more able to love them.

1
WHO NEEDS BABYSITTERS?

If you have a baby, or a child or children under the age of sixteen, the chances are that at some time or another you will need a babysitter.

The word 'babysitter' is a new one. It was never used before the 1930s, because the very idea of formal babysitting is a new one. Before extended families began to split up, before young couples began to pull up their roots and move about the country, things were different. At that time aunts and uncles, grandparents and cousins, grown-up brothers and sisters and their families frequently lived within a stone's throw of each other, usually in the communities where they were born, and the neighbours were as like as not old family friends. There was no need for professional babysitters. When the parents needed help with the children for any reason – perhaps because another baby was on the way, or there was severe illness or even death in the family – then the rest of the family, and the neighbours, too, rallied round and absorbed any children who needed looking after into their own homes. They didn't 'sit' with them as a full-time activity but simply gathered the children into the fabric of their own daily lives until they could return to their parents.

But the pattern of life has changed fundamentally since the Second World War, and few of us are lucky enough nowadays to have accommodating relatives in the next street. What's more, because very many mothers now go out to work, at least on a part-time basis, the *need* for child care has grown enormously. Society has therefore had to build up an artificial alternative to the loving care and cooperation once provided by the community as a matter of course. It has done this in many ways:

* voluntarily, with dozens of different community-based self-help babysitting systems;
* officially, with local authority child-care schemes;

11

* as part of the employment pattern, with nurseries at work;
* on a business level, with private nurseries, nursery schools and various other schemes.

Most parents need babysitters, but different parents have different needs. And it's also true that these needs will change from year to year. For instance, the young family with one parent at home and one out at work may become either a family of two working parents or a single-parent family in the future. The family which only needs occasional babysitting one year may need regular day care the next and 'latch-key' facilities later.

The Young Family

First of all, what are the needs of the young family with one parent at work all day and the other, usually but not always the mother, at home and fully occupied in looking after small children?

In this case the services of a babysitter are necessary to relieve the home-based parent of the companionship of little children and the resultant drain on her physical and mental energies. Maybe she needs nothing more than the occasional evening out – a chance to go to the theatre, the pub, a concert or dance, or just to spend a few relaxed hours with friends. However, she may need more. A few hours off during the day, even if it is just once a week, to shop in peace, or study, go swimming, learn to play a musical instrument . . . whatever she most needs to remind her that she is an individual with a mind and a life of her own and not just someone's mum. And it's just possible that if the opportunity arose she would positively blossom as a result of having a short holiday, even a brief weekend, away from her children. Family holidays can be fun, but they are almost always exhausting for the parents and therefore do little to refuel their energies or rebuild their frayed morale. We've discovered from experience that it works wonders for a young couple to be able to forget that they are *parents*, just for a little while, and to rediscover themselves, and each other, as *people*. And because their own relationship is enriched by the experience, the chances are that their relationship with their children will be, too.

12

The Family with Two Working Parents and Children Under Five

The second group that needs babysitters – but on a much more regular basis – is that of families in which both parents go out to work, either full-time or part-time, and have children who don't yet go to school. These parents depend entirely on being able to find trustworthy, continuous babysitting – or child-minding, nurseries or whatever – on which they can totally rely, day in, day out, the whole year through. Otherwise their jobs are in jeopardy.

The Family with Two Working Parents and School-Age Children

The next group is made up of families in which both parents go to work and the children are all at school. Their needs are often complex. For the bulk of the time, if the children are healthy and especially if one parent finishes work reasonably early in the afternoon, they may be able to manage without help. But then they may suddenly face the complication of a sick child who needs care during the day or is unexpectedly at home for any one of a host of reasons. They will certainly have a problem when the long school holidays start. Although some working parents manage to get home by the time their children come in from school, a very large number cannot. A *Woman's Own* survey carried out in 1979 showed that in a quarter of homes with working mothers and school-age children neither mum nor dad was at home when school finished.

The Single-Parent Family

Another group that nearly always needs help in looking after the children – and often has very little money to spend on child care – is single-parent families. One out of every eight British families has only one parent; 920,000 families are bringing up one-and-a-half *million* children. There are also many families which technically have two parents, but work or other factors keep them apart.

Even if the single parent doesn't go out to work, he – or more often she – still needs some time away from the children. If this is important for a married parent, it is even more vital for a parent alone who has to cope with the daily struggle of being both mother and father, often on a limited income, and who rarely has anyone with whom to share either the physically exhausting side of parenthood or its worries and emotional demands. Just having someone to listen when little Jacky has been putting chewing gum in Jane's hair *again,* or Billy's bad language is getting even *worse*, can make the matter seem less important and easy to laugh off. But keeping everything bottled up can turn a trivial matter into a nightmare. So any single parent needs the occasional services of a babysitter, even if just for a natter with a friend.

If a single parent has to go out to work as well, then she really will need as much help with child care as she can possibly get, at a price she can afford. Otherwise both she and her children will suffer.

The Family in Emergency

Unlike single-parent families, some families normally need very little help. Perhaps the mother is at home most of the time anyway, and when she does want some time off someone nearby is quite happy to 'sit' for her. But a situation which seems secure and well organized can change drastically at a time of crisis. If the mother is ill, or if one of the children has to go into hospital and needs a parent with her, for instance, it may well be difficult to find proper care for the children left at home. An understanding employer may give the father time off to take care of the household. But unfortunately not all employers are understanding, and not all fathers believe that their place could possibly be in the home, whatever the crisis. So emergency short-term babysitting of some sort may be vital.

The Family with a Handicapped Child

Finally, this is one other group which is in very great need of babysitting and child care, but because of the condition of their children they may find it extremely difficult to get. The very factor that makes them need help so desperately makes that help hard to come by. Recent estimates reveal that in the UK there are 200,000 moderately handicapped children and a further 44,000 severely handicapped children, and most of these are cared for in their own homes.

The nervous and physical strain of looking after a disabled child can be enormous. Her needs and demands can be devastating to both mind and body, even if she is immensely lovable and deeply loved. For these families, therefore, a babysitter can be a life-line, the only factor keeping the parents from nervous or physical breakdown.

In short, babysitting has become a basic requirement for our twentieth-century well-being, that of the children as well as the parents. And it is important to realize that needing the services of a sitter or childminder is not 'bad'. If properly planned, and the children well prepared, the experience can be positive and enriching for everyone involved. The mother who manages to remind herself that there's more to life than nappies can go home refreshed and more devoted to her children than ever. The child who spends the day with a minder who is prepared to play games, lets the child help with the baking, takes her to the park and provides her with toys and books, can return home filled with zest and excitement, plus a new fund of ideas and experiences. One friend of ours, a young mother with a happy family life who also enjoys a high-powered job, says of her three-year-old's relationship with her childminder: 'She really *loves* going to her – I believe she'd get dreadfully bored just here in the flat with me all day long!'

One word of warning. Children can thrive and flourish under all sorts of child-care arrangements, whether in their own home or someone else's, with a childminder, or in a nursery or a playgroup, provided that they *know* beyond a shadow of a doubt that they can rely on the constant love of at least one particular adult. And in most cases, though by no means all, that will be their mother. So if you have to leave your child in care for long hours, make sure that when you *do* manage to get together she feels she has your complete and unwavering love and support. No matter how hard it is, you should always find time for her. This is vitally important. You cannot begin cleaning the house, cooking or organizing your social life, or even sitting down with your feet up, until she has first been welcomed back to you. This is her *right*, and it can be your joy.

An insecure child who feels unloved may show symptoms of distress, among them bed-wetting, thumb-sucking or silent, solitary rocking. But there are many, many more. Take notice, and take action. Cuddles, comfort and loving care are called for, and if they don't do the trick you may need to see your doctor or seek other professional advice.

2
INDIVIDUAL BABYSITTERS:
from Neighbours to Au Pairs

Parents' most common need is for occasional evening babysitters and for the odd hour of supervision during the daytime.

The Freelance Babysitter

For the most part there are two kinds of freelance babysitters: teenage children of friends and neighbours who do the job occasionally for a little extra pocket money, and more experienced people who do it regularly, are more expensive, and provide a professional service.

Though we refer throughout this book to babysitters as 'she', it is important to point out that male sitters are quite as adept as women in this field. Many parents worry unnecessarily. They may be afraid to ask a man to change nappies when he would be perfectly willing and able to do so.

It is usually best to use the same sitter regularly and build up a good stable relationship. She may be a student, a young unemployed person, or just someone trying to make some extra money. If possible use one you know or who has been recommended by a friend. Alternatively, you may see an advertisement in a shop window or decide to advertise on your own account. You could put up a card in a newsagent's shop or on the students' notice board of a nearby college or hostel. Or you could use the local newspaper. Shop window advertisements should be neat and eye-catching.

BABYSITTER WANTED
about 1 evening per week
£x per hour
1 Bunting Rd,
Belfast 7
Tel: 246 8000

An advertisement in the local newspaper costs little compared with the hours of babysitting you stand to gain from it. The wording should be concise: '**BABYSITTER** wanted. Occasional evenings. £x per hour. Apply 1 Bunting Road, Belfast 7. Tel: 246 8000.' You could add 'male or female' if you are happy with either.

Don't offer to pay fares, because you should be trying to attract someone who lives nearby. This saves transport problems and makes it easier for you to get in touch with her and persuade her to come in an emergency or to do occasional late 'sits'. This is why you should include the name of your street in the advertisement, even if you are hoping applicants will telephone you.

You might also want to include some details about the child or children. For instance, if you have only one and she would usually be asleep, say so: 'One child, little attention needed'. This may attract a reliable student who needs time to study. But you should be aware that emergencies do happen and even the best behaved of children occasionally wake up when they're not expected to, and make sure that the sitter is confident she can cope if necessary. If you have a couple of lively monsters who need a lot of attention, it's better to come clean and admit it. You may attract a sitter who loves playing with children. Anyway, there's no point in trying to conceal the facts; it will just take one evening's babysitting to reveal the truth, and what you are looking for is a long-term babysitter, not a series of one-nighters.

You can easily find out from friends in the neighbourhood or the sitters themselves what the going rate of pay is. It may seem to you rather a lot for the little work involved, but try to be generous. This will encourage the sitter to be available and pay dividends in an emergency. If you can't afford long 'sits' you may find younger babysitters who are quite happy to look after your children just for a couple of hours – long enough for you to meet friends for a drink or go for a walk.

If you get a lot of replies to your advertisement it is a good idea to choose a shortlist of two or three willing people who between them should be able to cope with most of your babysitting needs. But don't use too many as some children find a succession of new faces worrying. Ask the best of those who reply to pop in to meet you and the children, and also to supply you with a reference. Anyone who is not prepared to do either should be viewed with suspicion. Do follow up their references. All you need to know is whether they are honest, good-tempered and reliable. If you don't check up you will only have yourself to blame if any valuables disappear or you come home to a distressed baby.

It should not be difficult to choose the babysitters you and your children like most, but keep in mind that a shy, diffident person, or someone who doesn't seem genuinely interested, might seriously worry a child whereas a firm and authoritative sitter could project a sense of reliability. One father told us, 'Frankly, *I* thought our babysitter was fearfully bossy and overbearing, but Libby *loved* her. Even the little boy downstairs came running up to be minded whenever she was here!' Once you have made your choice of babysitters, take the precaution of keeping the details and telephone numbers of any others who seem competent in case you need to fall back on them. Babysitting circles are discussed in Chapter Eight.

Another source of babysitters is your local Social Services department, which may be able to put you in touch with capable but partially physically handicapped people who might relish the idea of being useful and in contact with lively young people. They may also know of retired people in the area who want to do light work.

The Babysitting Agency

Occasional evening babysitters can also be found through agencies. Perhaps the only advantage is that a sitter is nearly always available. It cannot be assumed that the sitter will be experienced or vetted by the agency, and you will not necessarily get the same sitter every time.

Agencies cost slightly more than freelance sitters. The fee is usually the same as that of a freelance professional, but on top of that a membership fee is usually charged, of about the equivalent of eight hours' babysitting fees. For this an agency undertakes to supply a sitter for any evening, unless perhaps you try to book one at the very last minute. A lift home or taxi fare is insisted upon after 11 pm, and the minimum booking is usually four hours.

The agency sitter has to pay a percentage of the fee you give her back to the agency. Many parents feel she is exploited, but of course the agency does give her a form of protection as well as regular work, and no-one could become rich on the money involved. If you make a private arrangement for a sitter to return to you without either of you informing the agency, and it is discovered, she will probably be fired.

Rich parents complain at least as often as poor ones about paying an extra few pence, and people often give a pound for a taxi ride which they fully realize will cost two. The embarrassed sitter will probably quietly accept it and then walk half her journey home in order not to deplete her earnings. This haggling will win parents nothing in the end though, as the agency may mark them down as a 'bad sit' and the sitter will refuse to return in any case.

A personal relationship may not develop with an agency sitter, but some parents prefer this simple business-like arrangement. It is still worthwhile being pleasant and friendly. If she is not treated well by you she may not devote quite so much care and consideration to your children. Usually she is expected to give her earnings for the first full hour to the agency but is allowed to keep the rest, so if you can afford to tip her it will be hers to keep.

Agencies may be found through the Yellow Pages of the telephone directory, listed under Employment Agencies and Specialists. Local newspapers may also carry small ads under Household Services or Personal. If an agency is to be chosen as one of your systems, it might be worth your while to ask them what services they provide – daytime sitting, for instance – before you make your choice.

Occasional Daytime Sitters

It is not as easy to find sitters for daytime care, as obviously this is a rather more demanding job and unless payment is higher it does not seem very attractive. Also, many evening babysitters cannot be available during the day. However, there are bound to be some among the sources already recommended, especially retired people, who would enjoy playing with children for a couple of hours on an occasional basis. And once you've found someone suitable, it might be worth trying to rearrange your own schedule to fit in with her available times. If you advertise you should make it clear whether you want help for odd days or for the same morning or afternoon each week.

Agencies Some babysitting agencies can help in the daytime, but not all. However, they *may* be able to introduce you to someone who lives nearby and who might be prepared to help out, so it is worth trying them.

Childminders These are usually used as a system of regular child care, but some are willing to take on occasional minding. The best procedure for finding one who is properly qualified is described in the next section.

Babysitting circles (see Chapter Eight) In most cases these can be easily adapted to fit in with daytime needs. Some people will enjoy doing sits in the afternoon to build up a pool of returned sits for their evenings out.

So, though finding a day sitter may not be easy, it is not impossible, and a little perseverance will almost certainly solve your problem. For those parents who can afford more regular day care, individual help is provided by:

★ a childminder
★ a nanny
★ a mother's help
★ an au pair
★ a mother's help/au pair
★ paired au pairs

These alternatives are very different from each other. They tend to vary in the nature of the care they give, the hours they offer, the fees they charge, and even the sort of children they accept. And some are easier to find in one part of the country than another. Some live in your home, others come in on an hourly basis, and still others look after your child in their own home.

The Childminder

Since day nurseries are in such short supply, childminders have sprouted like the flowers in May to fill the gap. A childminder is defined as anyone, apart from a close relative, who takes care of a child under five for two hours or more in any one day, in her own home, and gets paid for it. In this country approximately half a million children are looked after by minders. Yet in the 1974 Office of Population Censuses and Surveys statistics it was revealed that only 3% of mothers *wanted* their children to be looked after by minders, and that of those using them, 73% would have preferred some other form of care.

The fact is, there *are* some very good minders. Working people from every conceivable walk of life have found that the system works wonderfully for them. Their bright, happy and secure children prove the point. However, there are some very bad childminders, and these are the ones you must take great pains to avoid.

Childminders should be registered with the local authority – this is a legal requirement. Though registration does not, in itself, guarantee a high quality of child care, and consequently there are moves to have it either abolished or made much more stringent, as things stand at the moment it acts as a slight safeguard. We would not advise you to use an unregistered childminder. There may be some sinister reason why she hasn't applied for, or been given, registration. For instance, her house may not be properly protected against fire hazard; she may have a history of violence or be considered medically unfit. If a childminder *is* registered it means that she has been visited by a health visitor or social worker who has talked to her, looked around her house and checked the facilities she can provide to make sure they are acceptable as far as warmth, cleanliness and comfort are concerned. The number of children she is allowed to take care of at one time has been fixed according to the facilities. Her home has been checked to see that it is safeguarded against accidents, and she has been examined to make sure that she is of good health and character.

Unfortunately, this supervision is often cursory. And, of

course, unscrupulous minders can put on a good show for visitors but behave very badly when they have gone. There is now an attempt, spearheaded by the National Childminding Association, to give childminders some form of basic training and advice so that they realize their job is an important one and learn how to do it well.

You can get a list of registered minders in your area from the social services department. It is also worth asking a health visitor or friends with children whether they can recommend a good childminder who may have vacancies, or you could make enquiries at the baby clinic. Before you entrust your baby to a minder, even a recommended one, you should always go to see her and, if possible, meet other children in her care. You should ask her a few searching questions – *and* satisfy yourself that you are getting honest answers. Here are a few which might be helpful:

★ How many children do you look after, and what are their ages?
★ Is there a safe and pleasant garden where they can play?
★ What sort of outings do you arrange for them, and how often?
★ How much room is there in the house where they can play?
★ What books and play equipment do you have for them?
★ Is there somewhere for them to rest?
★ Would you be prepared to take them to a playgroup or toy library?
★ Will you be cooking a hot lunch for them?

If you can find a good childminder this may be the best solution for your child. She will have a chance to build up a close relationship not only with a second mother figure but also, perhaps, with the minder's family, and for an only child in particular this can be a great treat. She will not be swamped by too many people or confused by too many different faces, as sometimes happens in a day nursery where the helpers often work shifts and do not have a chance to develop a personal relationship with the children in their charge. She will have a much more flexible timetable, for routine can be less rigid within a family than an official set-up. And she will feel that she *belongs*.

The amount you pay your childminder normally depends upon a private arrangement between the two of you. As a general guide, in 1980 the rate in London was £16 for a full week. If you pay a minder well she tends to feel more respect for herself and the work she is doing. If you treat her kindly and considerately, as a friend and supporter rather than an employee, that kindness will be transferred to your child.

If you are working but still cannot afford a fair rate for childminding, examine your financial situation very carefully. It may be that you would be better off staying at home, living on social security, and spending more time with your child. If you feel her happiness and safety are at risk, don't feel guilty about choosing such an alternative. For help with this very common dilemma a wonderful service is provided by counsellors at the Child Poverty Action Group (see Directory of Useful Organizations). Gingerbread (also in the Directory) will guide you through the intricacies of claiming all the benefits provided by the welfare state.

The Nanny

The most expensive and highly-qualified child care is provided by that magnificent British institution, the nanny.

The nannies most in demand these days tend to be those who are trained by the private nursery training colleges affiliated to the Association of Nursery Training Colleges. The most famous of these is 'Norlands' or, to give it its full title, the Norland Nursery Training College. Norlands Nannies are renowned the world over because of the college's careful selection of students, training and high standards.

Would-be nannies entering a private nursery training college are normally required to have a few O-level passes before they are accepted, and to be at least eighteen years old. Many will have had some experience of child care before they become students. They then spend eighteen months or two years being trained in all aspects of the care of children from birth to seven years old. Part of the training is theoretical and part of it practical, performed with children in nurseries attached to the colleges or in private families. The students work towards a college diploma as well as the certificate awarded by the National Nursery Examination Board (the NNEB) – the basic nanny qualification. Student nannies can also take the Nursery Nurses' Diploma Examination given by the Royal Society of Health as an extra qualification.

However, not all nannies are trained at private colleges. There are two-year courses administered by local authorities which also lead to the NNEB qualification, and girls can be accepted for these even if they don't possess any academic qualifications. Students spend two days per week on practical training – in nurseries, nursery classes, and so on – and three days a week at a college of further education, where they study all aspects of child care and child development as well as continuing their general education.

Some nannies, of course, do not possess paper qualifications. They may have had experience as an au pair, a mother's help, or simply as one of a large family. If they enjoy working with children and have sufficient good sense to do it very well, one of these may suit your needs admirably and cost you less.

There are many ways of obtaining a nanny. You can use an agency – look under Employment Agencies and Specialists in the Yellow Pages of the telephone directory. Or you can reply to an advertisement, or advertise yourself, in *The Lady* magazine or in *Nursery World*. Another good idea is to advertise in the national press or in local papers. If you advertise in those areas where unemployment is especially high, you may attract dozens of applicants – though those who reply to local advertisements may not have the same professional expertise as the job-hunters searching through the employment columns of the specialist child-care magazines.

If you are going to spend money on an advertisement, spend a little extra and have it boxed off in what is called a 'semi-display' so that it will attract attention. Don't waste too many words on saying things like 'own room and TV' – nannies take those things for granted nowadays. Try instead to give a personal flavour to the advertisement. Give your address, too, rather than a box number, so that applicants will have some idea of where you would want them to live.

NANNY
(over. 20)
for **ELLEN**
(12 weeks)
Mum is an air hostess
so hours irregular.
Friendly, informal
household in Sutton.
Tel: 123 4567.

Obviously you will have to interview applicants very carefully before you decide who is right for your baby. Her job will be to take complete charge of the child. She will look after her, talk to her, read to her, play with her, take her for walks and outings, teach her to do things for herself, prepare her food, do her laundry, and perhaps clean the nursery. Therefore she needs to be energetic, efficient, responsible, sensible and safety-conscious. But she needs to be much more than that. She needs to be affectionate, imaginative, resourceful, cheerful, sympathetic to a child's demands upon her *and* to share your own ideas of what is important in the way children are cared for and brought up. Here are some of the questions you might ask her to help you make up your mind as to whether she will fill the bill.

★ What sort of toys do you think a child should have?

★ What are your favourite books for reading aloud to children?

★ What games do you most enjoy playing with children?

★ If you took the child out for a walk, where would you take her? Would you talk to her? What sort of things would you show her?

★ What do you feel about children watching television?

★ Do you believe in slapping small children?

★ How would you cope with a temper tantrum?

★ If the child began to cry and couldn't be pacified, how would you cope?

★ Do you believe in a strict routine and timetable, or do you prefer a more flexible pattern?

★ What would you do if the child fell and bumped her head badly? swallowed a button? cut her hand severely? was very sick? (etc.)

If you find a nanny whom you like and respect, treat her with care and consideration. She will need regular time off – at least one full day a week, and two weekends a month. One or two guaranteed free evenings a week should also be granted, but most families allow their nannies to go out on any evening that they themselves are at home. She will expect to have her own room, and a bathroom which she will share with the children. She will also ask, as a rule, for her own television, gas ring and/or electric kettle, and washing machine. As a rule she will expect to take most of her meals with you, but in many families the nanny has her evening meal in her own room so that both she and the family can organize their separate evening activities. However, the arrangements are best made to suit individual preferences – there is no need for hard-and-fast rules.

If you want to keep your nanny, *never* make the mistake of confusing her with a mother's help. The chances are she will flare her well-bred nostrils and depart. A highly-qualified nanny is a trained professional who respects herself and her profession. Her job is purely to look after the child, *not* to do the housework, family cooking, laundry, cleaning, or whatever. At her job she is excellent, but as a rule she will not contemplate doing anything other than her job.

A cheaper and sometimes more convenient way of employing a nanny is to find one who lives nearby and who is prepared to come in on a daily basis, arriving at breakfast time and departing when the baby is tucked up in bed. To find a daily nanny you could advertise locally. Alternatively, contact the local authority, find out if it runs an NNEB course, and then put an advertisement on the notice board of the appropriate college in the summer term when some of the students will be coming to the end of their training.

Be warned that usually there aren't enough nannies to go round. Good ones are normally in very short supply. So not only will you have to work hard at finding one in the first place, but then you'll have to work hard at *keeping* her.

Those who hanker after a nanny but feel that such a luxury is beyond their means may be interested in a 'Share-A-Nanny' scheme. This basically simple idea matches two sets of parents who employ one nanny between them. The nanny may care for up to four children from two families. The system works well provided that the parents are prepared to be flexible.

The Mother's Help

If you don't feel grand enough, or rich enough, to engage a nanny – or even half a nanny – you may be able to find a mother's help, who will not have a nanny's qualifications and will not therefore expect to be as highly paid. Nor will she have a nanny's attitude to housework. She will expect to help with all the jobs that are normally those of a stay-at-home mother, whether reading stories or washing dishes. But if you wish to keep her don't expect too much or overload her with chores. Better by far that she should look after the children well and earn their affection and trust than rush around all day trying to keep the windows shining and the cooker spotless. Expect her to be a *help*, not a miracle-worker.

Quite a lot of women who apply for jobs as mother's helps are, in fact, mothers themselves, with a young child in tow. They are either looking for a day job to which they can take the baby along so that *they* don't have the problem of finding babysitters or day care; or they may be single parents looking for a roof over their heads and offering a useful form of help in return. This sort of arrangement can work extremely well – or it can spell disaster. Again, it's a matter of temperament, motivation and all sorts of other imponderables. Before you become too deeply involved, try to get to know your prospective home-help pretty well and make sure you get some sort of character references. If all seems in order you should still play safe and suggest a trial period which will be a safeguard for *all* of you, mothers and children. But don't react with a blanket negative – you may be cutting yourself off from an immensely useful assistant and the opportunity for you and your child to make rewarding new friendships.

The Au Pair

The nature of an au pair's role and contribution to a household, and the terms under which she comes into this country, are closely defined by the Home Office (see Directory). For instance, she must be female, aged seventeen to twenty-seven inclusive, unmarried and without dependants, and a national of a Western European country including Cyprus, Malta and Turkey. She will be allowed to spend a total of no more than two years in an au pair capacity, and she will be expected to pay her own fare to get here. She will not be allowed to take a proper job. If she does so, both she and you may be breaking the law.

Her aim will be to learn the English language by living for a time with an English-speaking family as one of the family, and in return for this she will help the family *as* one of the family and *not* as a domestic servant. She will normally expect the household to include at least one adult woman, usually referred to as 'the hostess', unless she is told in advance that it does not.

There are various ways of finding an au pair – sometimes this is done through personal knowledge of her family, or through a church or social organization, or advertisement. Alternatively you could choose one of the agencies recommended by the Federation of Personnel Services Ltd (see Directory).

An agency is required to give you full details of the au pair, including the name and address of her next of kin, and they may ask you both to sign a written agreement for between six months and a year. But before you reach that stage they will let you interview a candidate if she is already in the country, and some of them will arrange a trial period of about twelve days to see how you get on together. They will, of course, charge you a fee for a successful placing, of between £30 and £60 at 1980 rates.

You are able to expect of your au pair that:
★ she will live with you as a grown-up daughter, sharing your life-style and family habits to some extent, and
★ she will be prepared to take a share in the light housework jobs you normally do yourself for up to about five hours a day, including looking after young children, and to give up about two evenings a week to babysit for you, making up to about thirty hours altogether.

She can expect from you:
★ generous pocket money – about £15 at 1980 rates, but of course, you'll need to take inflation into account;
★ her own room where she can study in comfort. It should be

warm and pleasant and furnished with an armchair, upright chair, table or desk with lamp, and a bookcase, as well as her bed, dressing table and storage facilities for her clothes and belongings;

★ some help in finding local classes where she can improve her English;

★ the opportunity to go to religious services if she wishes, to have a certain amount of social life, and to be able to visit places of interest. You may have to help her to make friends and meet people of her own age at the beginning – this can often be very difficult;

★ at least one *fixed* day off each week when she is completely free from any sort of domestic work.

Do be aware, *before* you launch into making the arrangements, that the relationship between an au pair and her hostess can be a difficult one for some people and requires a certain amount of adjustment. Each of you will have to make allowances for the other. The job may well be her first since leaving school, and she is in an awkward situation. She wants to feel free and independent – that is why she wants to leave home and travel – yet she is still in the position of a daughter with someone responsible for her, so her 'freedom' is curtailed. She may speak little English and find it difficult to communicate these conflicting emotions, or to explain the homesickness and insecurity which will probably upset her occasionally. Though living as one of the family, she may feel very much a stranger, and though she wants to feel very grown up she may, in reality, be more dependent upon you than a daughter of your own would be.

You, on your part, have to adjust to having a newcomer share your kitchen, bathroom and so on, and be present in the intimate areas of domestic life. Family rows and tensions may have to be controlled and freedom of expression slightly restricted if she is not to be embarrassed or upset. You must make her welcome in your living room and at your dining table and encourage her both to find friends *and* invite them into your home; otherwise you'll have no-one but yourself to blame if she goes around looking bored and dejected. You'll also have to keep a maternal eye on her love-life. If she seems particularly young and vulnerable, you might ask her to let you know at what sort of time she is planning to come home so that you know what to expect and can take some action if the unexpected happens. It is not a good idea to let her stay out all night unless you know where she's going to be, and if you can tactfully ask her about her friends so much the better. In other words, treat your *young* au pair just as you would like a hostess in a foreign country to treat your own daughter. Of course, if she's obviously well able to look after herself, and even to teach you a thing or two, you don't need to have the same compunction.

However, if she does get into trouble of any kind, you should get in touch with her family, her consulate, or the local Citizens' Advice Bureau. If she decides to leave you, do make sure that she has somewhere to go and enough money to get there. If she leaves without giving you her new address, you should tell the Home Office.

Au Pairs Travelling from Abroad

If through advertising or some organization you have found a girl who is still in her own country, then first of all send her as much information as you possibly can about your home and circumstances. You could either write a detailed letter or make a copy of the following form and fill it in for her. You could also send her some photographs of the family, pets, house and garden, etc.

Au Pair Arrangements for:
1. Name of host and hostess:
   Address and telephone number:
   Nationality:
   Husband's occupation (full or part-time):
   Wife's occupation (full or part-time):
   Religion:
   Language normally spoken in the home:
2. *Household*
   Ages:
   Sex:
   Relationship:
   Domestic help (hours per week):
   Domestic animals:

3. *Accommodation*
   House/flat:
   Number of rooms:
   Number of bathrooms:
   Central heating:
4. *Location*
   Distance from shopping centre (km/miles):
   Distance from public transport (km/miles):
5. *Facilities for English Language learning*
   Frequency of classes:
   Distance from home:
   Fees:
   Fares:
6. *Au Pair Duties*
   The sort of tasks you will be expected to assist with:
   How long, per day, these are likely to take:
   Free days:
   Frequency of babysitting:
7. *Pocket Money*
   £ per week:
8. *Period of stay*
   Begins: Ends:
9. *Travelling arrangements*

Make sure you tell her what sort of work you will expect her to do – e.g. take the children to school, walk the dog, go to the laundrette, get the children their tea, do the shopping – and give her simple but exact travel arrangements including the stage at which she will be met.

When she arrives in the UK she will be seen by an immigration officer (unless she is from the EEC) at the port or airport. She may have to have a medical examination and show her papers and correspondence with you. Then, provided that the officer is satisfied, she will probably have her passport endorsed to show that she has been given leave to stay for twelve months. If he is not satisfied, he may telephone you to check that all is as it should be.

Soon after she arrives at your house, ask her to show you her passport. If the endorsement shows that she is required to register with the police she must do so within seven days. She will have to go along to a police station taking with her her passport and two passport photographs and be prepared to pay a registration fee. It may help, especially if her English is weak, if you go along as interpreter and guide.

If she wants to stay longer than the period endorsed on her passport, she will have to apply to the Home Office before her time lapses, and she will need a letter from you to back her up.

You are not required to pay National Insurance for an au pair, and therefore she cannot claim sickness or other cash benefits. However, if she was paying Social Security contributions in her own country, she should ask the Department of Health and Social Security what her position is soon after she arrives. Note that she *can* obtain treatment under the National Health Service.

Au Pairs Plus

The law for foreign EEC nationals – girls from Belgium, Denmark, France, Italy, Germany, Luxembourg, Greece and the Netherlands – is rather different in that they *are* allowed to take employment in this country. Therefore you could use one of them as a mother's help/au pair, if you wished, and not be limited to the thirty-hour-week. But of course, if this is what you have in mind you *must* make it quite clear before she arrives, and you must be prepared to pay her considerably more than pocket money. You may find that you have to pay National Insurance contributions, and you should check this out from the Department of Employment.

Foreign au pairs can be great fun to have in the family – they learn about England and their hosts learn about their native land. Sometimes links are formed which lead to exchange holidays for the children or even the whole family. Pen-pal relationships may be established. And there's no doubt that young children often think it rather exciting having a foreigner in the household.

On the other hand, there's no reason at all why you shouldn't work out your own au pair-type system with a young girl or boy from this country. Stick to the same sort of rules about pocket money and time off, let them live as one of the family, and the arrangement can be a great success. Often it fits in very well for a student who wants to take a year off between school and university. Maybe she wants to do a part-time course of study in your town or city and would find it impossibly expensive to rent a bedsit. Alternatively, it is a very good way for any youngster to take that first step away from home, giving her some freedom and responsibility but also some support and family back-up. Your local social services department might have an ideal candidate to offer.

The Mother's Help/Au Pair

Again and again in our research into child-care arrangements we have discovered that the real success stories spring from flexible, informal arrangements where people help each other as and when the need arises in a spontaneous way – responding to the need instead of living by the rule book. Sometimes, however, rules are necessary, particularly to protect vulnerable people from being exploited or badly used, and it is for this reason that legislation exists governing the employment of au pairs.

An ordinary au pair is *not* the solution for a working mother who needs someone to look after her child full-time, five days a week, because she is only supposed to work *part*-time (approximately thirty hours a week) with ample time off to study the life and language of this country. However, some au pair agencies can also supply a mother's help/au pair who will work longer hours for larger wages, plus, of course, her keep. She will expect to have at least a day and a half off each week, as well as a few evenings. But if she is competent and easy to live with, and if she gets on well with you and the children, she may be the answer to your problem.

To find your mother's help/au pair you could contact the Federation of Personnel Services of Great Britain (see Directory) with your requirements, and they will put you in touch with suitable local agencies. Alternatively, look through the Yellow Pages of your telephone directory under Employment Agencies and Specialists.

If you prefer, you can advertise for a mother's help/au pair through a national newspaper, asking for detailed applications which will show you how much experience she has had with children, whether she can cope with the language, whether she is able and willing to cook, drive, and so on. Sift the letters carefully, then ask the most likely-sounding applicants to come along to be interviewed *and* to interview you. Of course, if they are living abroad you can hardly expect them to come to this country for an interview unless you are prepared to pay their fares. On the other hand, it is a bit of a risk engaging a girl whom you have never met. Arrangements are usually made for a period of six or twelve months, although a three-month summer visit can often be fixed.

Paired Au Pairs

Though at first glance it seems that basic au pairs cannot help the parent looking for full-time child care because of the laws governing the hours they work, there is a way round this problem which can be very successful, and though it's quite expensive it's not likely to be as expensive as a nanny. Instead of engaging one au pair, have two – preferably friends or sisters – and ask them to share the work between them. Girls often enjoy this arrangement because they have a companion and don't suffer the loneliness and strangeness that sometimes makes single au pairs give up and go home in despair. And the 'hostess' who is responsible for looking after them may find that they are much more able to look after themselves than if they were alone.

More informal arrangements are also possible, and these will of course be much less expensive but also much less reliable.

The Neighbour

It may be possible to find a neighbour who does not go out to work, and perhaps has a child at the same school as yours, who will be happy to look after your children through teatime and earn herself a little money in the process. Once this is established it may work for at least part of the holiday period as well, especially if the children are friends and in the habit of playing together. But don't take your neighbour for granted.

Basically she's doing you a favour, even though you are paying her for it. You probably need her more than she needs you. So treat her well, with understanding and consideration, and never ever exploit her kindness.

Rent-A-Gran

Sometimes sprightly pensioners living nearby would love the chance not only to earn a little extra money but also to spend some time in the company of children and be involved in a surrogate family. Often the young and the elderly get on very well together – the generation gap doesn't seem to gape so wide across fifty years as it does across twenty-five. You could try a 'Rent-a-Gran' advertisement in the local paper or corner shop. Alternatively, contact the social services department, some of which have registers of retired people who want to do light work.

Emergencies are always traumatic. And families with young children are particularly vulnerable to them, especially if one parent has to be responsible for the lion's share of the child care. If you are aware that your arrangements are rather fragile, take pains to prepare for a crisis beforehand so that if and when it happens you know exactly what to do.

The Social Services

Even the best-organized of families sometimes has to face emergencies that mean short-term care for the children. The most common crisis is the illness of the mother. In our experience the wisest course of action is to contact the social services department of your local authority immediately and ask for help (if there are no friends and relatives who are able to rally round). The sort of help they will provide will depend largely upon the nature of your crisis, the number of children who need care, and their own facilities. Probably the most useful thing they can do will be to send you a home-help – provided, that is, that you have someone around to help you in the evening. What you are charged for her services will vary according to where you live and your income. Alternatively, the social services department might suggest that it send the child/ren to a childminder or day nursery, or combine the services of a home-help and daily minder to make sure there is adequate care.

Not everyone realizes that some childminders are prepared to provide a temporary service, but this can be of enormous benefit to parents whose lives tend to be unsettled or whose work pattern is unconventional. For instance, an actress friend of ours tends to travel the country from one repertory company to another – and takes her two-year-old daughter with her. She contacts the social services department a short while before her rehearsal period begins and gets their list of childminders, then two or three days before she is due to start work she settles herself into digs, interviews her shortlist of minders to see which one is best for her baby, and makes sure that the child is quite settled before she starts work at the theatre. After the rehearsal period she is able to spend the day with her little girl and get a babysitter to look after her in the evenings. The arrangement seems to work: the child is contented and secure, the mother is able to act, earn, and have her daughter with her. And both of them are happy.

In extreme emergencies – especially in the case of a single-parent family without supporting friends or relatives – the children may be taken into care temporarily and either fostered for a few weeks in a private family or sent to a children's home.

The Voluntary Helper

There are one or two alternatives to relying on the support of the social services department. For single parents Ginger-bread (see Directory) may be able to help by putting you in touch with others who will help in a case of emergency. Check the telephone directory, Citizens' Advice Bureau or the library for the address of a local group.

Other voluntary organizations perform similar services. For instance Network, based in Watford, has an Emergency Mums scheme with a twenty-four-hour phone-in service for parents who have a crisis and need someone to look after their children. It may be worth enquiring at your local Citizens' Advice

Bureau whether there is a similar organization in your area. If there isn't, why not consider starting one when your personal crisis is over?

The Paid Helper

If money is no great object you can, of course, solve your problem by hiring a temporary nanny or home-help through an agency. Look them up in your telephone directory under Employment Agencies and Specialists, or look through the advertisements in *The Lady*, usually a rich fund of helpers of all sorts.

Whatever system of babysitting or child care you use, you should *always* have a back-up system. Never put all your eggs in one basket, or one day you'll find them all broken. Even the most loyal and reliable of babysitters can get the 'flu occasionally, fall in love or go on holiday. Even the most efficient of nurseries has to close its doors from time to time because of infection, lack of fuel or understaffing. Make sure, when things are going well, that if they go wrong you have a reserve babysitter lined up, the name of an agency which will help out at short notice, or the telephone number of an old friend who will temporarily step into the breach. Don't wait until the worst happens before you try to work out what to do – by then it will probably be too late.

3
GROUP FACILITIES:
from Nurseries to Playgroups

For babies and under-fives, regular organized child care away from home usually takes the form of:
* workplace nurseries
* day nurseries
* nursery schools
* nursery centres
* playgroups
* clubs

The Workplace Nursery

Workplace nurseries, or creches, may be found in local government offices, hospitals, factories, department stores or universities and colleges of education, where they have been set up by the employer or educational authority as a convenience for the women who work there. It would be a step forward if employers *and* women acknowledged that this is a service for *men*, too, and that child care is a matter of equal concern to mothers *and* fathers. In fact, under the Sex Discrimination Act of 1975, employers cannot discriminate between male and female employees in the provision of workplace nursery facilities for their children, yet fathers rarely ask to use those nurseries that are available except when their wives are ill or having another baby.

In many ways a creche at work seems to be the answer to every parent's prayer. It is usually subsidized by the employer. It eliminates the need for the complicated time and travel arrangements often required if the child is with a minder or nursery. It means that the parent can see her child during her lunch hour and tea-breaks, and she is on the spot if there is a sudden crisis. This can make for greater security and peace of mind all round. While we were doing our research a young woman executive admitted to us that she would go ahead and have a baby without delay if only her firm ran a workplace nursery. But without that provision she is postponing motherhood, convinced that the problem of finding satisfactory child care would almost certainly force her to give up her career or at least work at a lower level.

On the other hand, there are two major disadvantages. The child's pattern of life depends upon the parent's employment – so if mother loses her place with the firm baby loses her place in the creche. Many women admit that they find it very difficult to concentrate their minds and give their best to the job when their children are on the premises. With one ear cocked for familiar screams from the creche it is difficult to listen acutely with the other to the voice on the telephone. But it may be that this is largely a matter of temperament and the relationship between mother and child. It certainly does not apply to all mothers, and some only find their baby's presence distracting at first.

The evidence seems to suggest that with local government funds in short supply, the pressure will be placed more and more upon employers. If your employers do not provide a creche at present they may be open to persuasion (see Appendix). However, it must be realized that only when labour is in short supply is there a *great* deal of incentive for an employer to sponsor his own nursery. If he needs something to attract or keep staff he may find this a useful magnet. If not, he has nothing to lose by saying that only those parents who can organize their own day-care solutions need apply to him for work.

If you are hoping to find a job with a firm which already runs a creche – and if you don't feel that you have the energy to try to get one started – you should ask at your local Department of Employment whether there are any operating in your area.

The Local Authority Day Nursery

Some – but not enough – day nurseries are run by local authority social services departments. Since there aren't sufficient places to go round, those existing are usually offered on a priority basis to mothers who *have* to work for some reason. Occasionally they will take a child on a temporary basis if her mother has to go into hospital. The best way to get your child into a local authority day nursery is to get a health visitor, social worker or doctor to recommend your case to the social services office.

The hours the nurseries stay open vary from place to place and are not always ideally suited to the requirements of working parents. The children are cared for by people with nursery nurse training qualifications, *not* nursery teachers. Games and toys are provided but there is no attempt to teach the children. The charge made varies – it may range from a few pence to a few pounds a week. Unfortunately, the standard of care varies enormously, too, from the excellent to the frankly substandard, overcrowded and underequipped. And some nurseries are located in out-of-the-way places that are difficult to reach by public transport.

Make sure that any nursery is good enough for your child before you put her name down. If it *is* good but has no vacancies, it is still worth putting her name on the waiting list. It is just possible that a vacancy may come up before she is ready to start school.

The Private Day Nursery

There are also registered private day nurseries in Britain, more in the south than in the north. Legally they should be registered with the local authority, which may then keep an eye on their standards, staff and methods. You will be able to get a list of those in your area from the local social services department. Again, cost and quality vary enormously, and so do attitudes. Some are very strict and rigidly disciplined. Others have a more liberal approach to child care. Make sure you get the opportunity to see what their methods are and whether you approve of them before you entrust them with your child.

Because of the shortage of day nurseries, some local groups and voluntary organizations are beginning to set up their own. Organizations which have succeeded in this include the Church of England Children's Society, Save the Children and the London Nursery Campaign (see Directory). It might be worth popping into your local Citizens' Advice Bureau to find out whether any societies of this sort operate in your area.

Basically part-time care for young children is not as difficult to find as locating someone to look after them day in, day out, the whole year round. It is unlikely that a few hours here and there, perhaps just two mornings a week, will make it possible for you to go out to work, though it may tie in with a part-time job or home employment, or it could help a mother do some preliminary study as preparation for returning to her career or retraining. But this type of care certainly does make it easier for house-bound mothers to find a few hours in their busy week when they can be free to think of themselves rather than their families, and as such it is invaluable for their morale and happiness.

The Nursery School

Many local education authorities run free nursery schools or nursery classes attached to primary schools. Some nursery schools take children when they are two years old, but others will not accept them until they are three. Many just offer part-time education, taking different children in the mornings and afternoons. Some nursery classes take children when they are three, but others won't take them until they are four. Since they are part of the education system they do aim to *educate* – as opposed to day nurseries whose primary job is to *care for* the child – and they also keep normal school hours and holidays.

The Private Nursery School

Side by side with local authority nursery schools are private nursery schools. Some of these are very small-scale affairs, often run in private homes, and officially registered as nurseries with the local authority. Others are highly-organized, well-equipped schools with fully-qualified staff, and they are officially recognized as schools by the Department of Education. Standards vary enormously, and so do fees. Some are very expensive, and occasionally parents find themselves paying more for convenience or prestige than for a good introduction into the world of education for their children. The only *fixed* standards are a few basics, such as a certain number of loos, and fire and safety precautions. Before you entrust your child to one it is a good idea to go along and have a thorough look round, watch the other children at work and play, and ask the headteacher some searching questions. You should also ask local friends and neighbours their opinions – they may know something about the reputation of the place even if they haven't had direct experience with it.

You can find out about any private nursery schools in your area either by contacting the local education authority or by watching for their advertisements in the local paper. Or you could write to the British Association for Early Childhood Education (see Directory) for information and advice. The aim of this association is to work for the provision of sufficient nursery schools and classes. It has branches throughout the UK working closely with local education authorities and other local organizations. It also has strong links with day and residential nurseries, playgroups and childminders, and like many organizations in the field of child care it is in favour of further collaboration between the Department of Education and the social services in order to improve the provisions they make.

The Nursery Centre

A valuable extension to the nursery school is what local authorities call 'combined nursery centres' or, more neatly, 'children's centres'. These combine the aims and facilities of the day nursery with those of the nursery class and have the double function of 'caring' and 'educating'. They are jointly funded and administered by the local authority social services department and the Department of Education, and they employ both nursery nurses and teachers. They also do useful things like giving support to local playgroups, mother-and-toddler clubs and childminders, and they often organize clinics and toy libraries.

Nursery centres are obviously an ideal solution to the problems of many mothers. Unfortunately, their development has been hampered by the administrative difficulties arising from belonging to two departments, and there are many discrepancies between the wages, training and conditions of the two groups of workers. However, women should agitate for more nursery centres and demand an end to the divisions between these two government departments as far as child care is concerned (see Appendix).

If there is a nursery school or children's centre in your area you will be able to find out about it from the local education authority. By all means go along and see if you can enrol your child, but the chances are that she'll be put at the bottom of a very long waiting list. A wise parent makes sure of a place on the list while her child is still in the pram – if not in the womb! In some cases, if a child comes from cramped housing conditions or there is some distressing family problem, a health visitor or social worker may recommend priority, but nursery schools are not meant to be an antidote to social problems but an extra educational facility. This is an area of great controversy in spite of the fact that most educationists would argue that if a child is ever to recover from the educational disadvantages of spending her early years in a deprived household, it is absolutely essential that she be given extra educational benefits at as early an age as possible.

Though they vary in quality, nursery school standards are normally very high, and classes are kept small so that the teacher is able to give a lot of attention to every individual. They have excellent equipment and the environment is carefully planned to help the children extend their horizons, develop new skills, make friends, and begin to feel independent.

The Pre-School Playgroup

Because of the shortage of nursery schools and classes, playgroups have boomed during the last twenty years, largely under the auspices of the excellent Pre-school Playgroups Association (see Directory). The PPA's definition of a playgroup is: 'a group of three- to five-year-olds playing together regularly, several times a week, headed by a supervisor who may be trained, with the mothers taking an active part in the running'.

Because the regular care of under-fives is involved,

playgroups must be organized with the knowledge and approval of the local authority, so you can be sure that basic requirements of cleanliness and safety have been met. There is usually a small charge, but sometimes local authorities subsidize children in need. The hours vary from three hours every day to two mornings a week.

The Extended-Day Playgroup

Extended-day playgroups have now begun to operate in some places. By extending the hours and operating daily throughout the year, these groups *can* meet the needs of working parents. But to function properly they must have professional staff and therefore usually have to rely on financial assistance from local authorities. Nevertheless, recent figures showed that a place in an extended-day playgroup costs only a quarter as much as a place in a day nursery, so parents agitating for more provision could look into this idea (see Appendix).

The PPA now has a membership of over 13,000 playgroups. It has full-time workers, runs very helpful courses, and produces masses of useful literature. However, not all playgroups are run on PPA lines. Sometimes charities such as Save the Children (see Directory), as well as local authorities, run their own. Often they combine elements of nursery schools and day nurseries, and keep open for normal school hours. Though parents are welcome to join in if they wish, they don't have to, so these are probably more helpful to some women.

To find a playgroup in your area you could contact the Citizens' Advice Bureau, the health visitor, the social services department, or you could write to the PPA. If you *cannot* find a playgroup, you might consider starting one yourself (see Chapter Eight).

The Mother and Toddler Club

Both the PPA and local authorities are also involved in the provision of Mother and Toddler Clubs, where women can get together companionably while their children – usually limited to under-threes – play together. The benefits are great. The children learn how to be *social* creatures, sharing their toys with others, joining in games, becoming members of a group

45

instead of self-centred individuals. And for mothers there is the relief of just talking to others who may share common problems – feelings of isolation, loneliness, boredom or inadequacy. A Mother and Toddler Club can't directly help you get back to work – but it *can* help you to stay sane while you're a full-time mother.

If you think an MT Club might be a good idea and would be prepared to get together with a few friends to start one, get in touch with the PPA for help. Their booklet, 'Mother and Toddler Clubs – A Basis for Discussion', explains the necessary organization very clearly.

The Occasional Creche

Another useful form of child care is provided by occasional creches. These are sometimes run by the Area Health Authority in their Health Centres, Maternity and Child Welfare Centres. Often a local voluntary group will help supervise them and play with the children. Their aim is to give mothers a short break away from their two- to five-year-olds, allowing them time to be alone or with friends; to catch up with chores or relax completely. They also aim to help the child learn to mix easily with others and stimulate her interests, and are particularly useful for little ones with handicaps or speech difficulties. Sometimes a small charge is made, but this may be waived in cases of financial difficulty. Each session usually lasts about two and a half hours.

The local health visitor will know whether there is an occasional creche near you and when it is open. Many are organized on a simple 'walk-in' basis: you can just wander in and leave your baby with someone who knows how to look after her. You don't need to have booked or made any elaborate plans beforehand. But, of course, the operative word is 'occasional'. These creches are not for the parent who is looking for regular, continuous child care.

As children grow to school age their needs change and care is more difficult to organize, though it is every bit as vital to the physical, emotional and moral safety of the growing child.

Parents may be lulled into feeling that if the child is safe, warm and fed, she's OK. But she needs much more than that in her growing-up years if she's going to make the necessary adjustments to adult life.

In 1979 a Working Party on Latch-key Children was set up by the UK International Year of the Child Association. It revealed some frightening facts:

★ 225,000 five- to ten-year-olds and 300,000 eleven- to fifteen-year-olds are left alone after school each day.

★ At least 300,000 five- to ten-year-olds and 375,000 eleven- to fifteen-year-olds are left alone during school holidays.

★ Each month the NSPCC deals with some 230 cases of children actually put in danger by being left alone.

Their report pointed out that children needed latch-key schemes as much as their parents did, and urgently required somewhere safe and stimulating where they could play and experiment. And it went on to make four positive suggestions. It urged that the Government should:

★ recognize that the lack of provision for latch-key children is a serious problem;

★ acknowledge the cost effectiveness of supporting local groups to overcome the problem;

★ ensure adequate funding for viable voluntary projects providing after-school and holiday care; and

★ encourage education and social services departments to take joint responsibility for the provision of both statutory and voluntary after-school and holiday care.

There seems little point in arguing that children are their parents' responsibility, and that parents *should* be at home looking after them. A recent report from the NSPCC (see Directory) highlighted a worrying connection between poverty and baby-battering. Babies stand more chance of being battered if their parents are poor. Therefore it seems that if the only way a family can struggle above the poverty line is to have two working parents, a wise precaution would be to provide babysitting and childminding systems for their benefit. Presumably a latch-key child is less of a tragedy than a battered one, but a civilized society should be working hard to make sure that *neither* exists any longer.

Recently the Conservative Social Services Secretary, Patrick Jenkin, said, 'Ultimately it is for local authorities to assess what priority they can give to making provision for latch-key children, in the light of their overall assessment of priorities in their area'. So it is up to parents to tell them, very firmly, how *they* think their rates and taxes should be spent. In the meantime, since government money is in short supply, the shortfall in after-school and holiday care must come from other sources. The International Year of the Child Working Party estimated that it cost £10,000 a year to fund a good latch-key scheme, to pay for premises and at least one full-time paid member of staff. However, less expensive means could be found.

The Play Centre

Sadly, despite the fact that the need has been identified and the remedy suggested, very little has actually been done. In some cities, particularly the bigger ones, local education authorities operate a few play centres where children can go after school until about 6.30 pm and during the holidays from 9 am. Sometimes they provide light meals and lunches during the holidays, and a paid staff supervises the children and organizes games and entertainment. To find out if there is anything of this sort in your area contact the local education authority or the Citizens' Advice Bureau. Unless people ask, and keep on asking, facilities won't be offered.

The Workplace Nursery Play Centre

It may be possible for an established workplace nursery to absorb older children, in addition to its under-fives, without any huge extra financial outlay, and employees should press for this. There are model employers already providing the service who even lay on transport to get the children safely from school to the nursery, and these few should be given full credit for their initiative.

The Community Play Centre

There are other latch-key schemes – but again, not nearly enough – funded by special grants or charitable trusts or associations. Gingerbread, the association for single parents, runs 'Gingerbread Corner' at Croydon in Surrey. It is a model self-help project, looking after eighty five- to eleven-year-old children each day between 3 and 6 pm in term time and from 8.30 am to 6.30 pm during the holidays.

In this case the children are collected from neighbouring schools in a minibus and taken to a large Victorian house which has been converted especially to provide them with a relaxed, homely atmosphere. They are given tea and can play in the romp room or in the garden, or they can do their homework or sometimes watch television, until their parents arrive to collect them. They also spend their school holidays at Gingerbread Corner. Outings are arranged and they go swimming. They can play, paint, learn to cook, put on shows . . . whatever they fancy. And there are trained play-leaders and volunteers to supervise them.

A similar development – still very tiny but showing huge potential – is the 'Children's House'. Children's Houses take children after school, during weekends, and in holidays. A great range of play and leisure activities are safely supervised by friendly, experienced adults. So far there are very few of them – only seven throughout the country at the last count – but more are in the pipeline and it is to be hoped that the idea will catch on and grow quickly. The experience of setting up imaginative play centres means the Children's House Society (see Directory) can give good advice.

It is sad, though, that both Gingerbread Corner and Children's Houses are planned only for the five-to-eleven age group. Many parents of older children would be delighted to see these ideas extended to cope with the complex needs of young teenagers. It is, in fact, comparatively easy to start your own after-school and holiday scheme, since the stringent rules applied by social services departments to the care of under-fives don't apply to older children. All you need is a *place* – perhaps just a back bedroom – and a tiny *budget*. Once you've done it you've proved that the need exists and that you can meet that need, and you are therefore likely to get further funds and help if you apply for them (see Appendix).

Organized holidays or playschemes help. They can be

home-based or residential, but they don't normally last long enough to occupy the entire holiday, so most of them can just be regarded as a bonus rather than a solution (see Chapter Five). There are lots of clubs to join – sports clubs, for instance, specializing in athletics, tennis, swimming, judo or squash. Or children could become members of a sports centre and enjoy a variety of sports. To find out where your nearest sports club or centre is, look under Sports Grounds, Playing Fields and Stadiums in the Yellow Pages of the telephone directory. Or ask the Citizens' Advice Bureau or the local library, or write to the National Playing Fields Association (see Directory).

Those less sportingly inclined might prefer a different sort of club, for instance amateur theatre, disco dancing, music making, handicrafts or art. The reference department of the library will know what is available. And, of course, there are Youth Clubs, Scouts, Guides and church groups in most villages and towns.

But again, the provision is not enough to meet the need. In 1973 a new scheme was launched to encourage facilities for all forms of play and recreation for children, called Fair Play For Children (see Directory). Its aims are to persuade government to provide the sort of play space and equipment children and young people need; to make them face the tragic cost of child death and injury on the roads, building sites, waste ground and rubbish dumps and to invest in play facilities on a major scale as the only logical answer. At the centre of its campaign is an action programme to persuade education authorities to allow schools, school grounds and facilities to be used for the benefit of children out of school hours. You can find out more about their work by writing to them for a copy of their report, *Why Lock Up Our Schools?*

4
CHOOSING THE BEST

With all the difficulty of trying to find care or babysitting for your child, the temptation is to feel that so long as you find someone someplace to look after her, your problem is solved. That's not true, of course. It's not just child care you're looking for – it's *good* child care.

The early years of childhood are enormously important. Look after her properly, feed her curiosity, extend her horizons, develop her interests, encourage her independence, and give her lots of love – physical cuddling as well as emotional support – and the chances are that your child will grow up into a happy, well-balanced, competent adult. Stint any of these, and she may have problems. To provide all that is no small undertaking, but there are further considerations. Do you approve of an ordered life-style, based on discipline and authority, or would you rather encourage individualism and self-expression even if it leads to a certain amount of chaos? Do you think formal education should begin early, or would you prefer to see your child spend her first years in play and exploration?

What about your own child's temperament and needs? Is she a solitary little girl who desperately needs other children to help her to socialize and overcome her shyness, or is she overpowered by other people if not given some personal attention and individual care? Is she a lively, bustling extrovert who needs constant activity and the opportunity to let off steam – or is she quiet, with a deep need to be alone occasionally to think her own thoughts and do her own thing?

All these considerations must be considered when you are doing the rounds of playgroups, day nurseries, and nursery schools and classes in your area. And if it's a childminder you're after, it is even more important to make sure that you know what your child wants and needs at this critical stage in her development.

As one mother told us, 'Finding the right childminder is basically a matter of *chemistry*. In some cases there's an instant rapport between the minder and Yvette. Something clicks, they understand each other and you know at once that everything's going to be all right. But in others, Yvette looks at the minder and the minder at Yvette and there's nothing there, nothing at all. If they knew each other all their lives they'd still be strangers. And that's just no good.' So the *right* care is much more than a mere matter of hygiene and safety, but both of these factors have to be taken into account.

Hygiene and Safety

Registered childminders, playgroups, local authority nurseries and registered private nurseries should be checked out by the local council to make sure that they reach certain basic standards – though the strict rules about premises where under-fives are cared for do not apply to those for school-age children. Anyway, standards sometimes slip and checks aren't always as thorough as they might be, so it must be repeated that you should satisfy *yourself* on these two counts before you go any further.

It would be totally unrealistic – and undesirable, too – to expect the premises to be as sterile and hygienic as an operating theatre. Humans can be messy creatures, and our bodies, fortunately, can withstand a certain amount of dirt. On the other hand, children in groups are particularly prone to a whole range of childhood infections and illnesses, and some of these, like gastric enteritis, can be quite devastating to the very young, so some precautions are essential. Do make sure that there are sufficient lavatories, that these are kept clean, that there are washing facilities close at hand *and* that the children are encouraged to use them whenever they go to the toilet.

If the children eat at the nursery or playgroup make sure that the kitchen is clean and well equipped and that there is proper provision for keeping food fresh and refrigerated if necessary. Contaminated food is a very common cause of illness, especially in warm weather.

It is also vital that the premises are safe, and that the proper precautions have been taken as far as fire risk is concerned. The statistics about accidents in the home make terrifying reading. For example, over six hundred children die as a result of accidents in the home in the UK every year.

Don't forget that the home in question could be yours. Safety precautions should not only apply to childminders' homes, nurseries and playgroups — *any* house sheltering young children should be carefully and regularly checked for danger. The biggest threats to children indoors are:
* choking and suffocation
* burns and scalds
* falls and cuts, and
* accidental poisoning

in that order. The following set of safety rules should be observed in any house where your child is accustomed to play.

The Safety Dozen

* Check that there are *fixed* guards on all fires;
* no electric flex is allowed to hang down from kettles, electric casseroles, toasters, etc.;
* saucepan handles are not allowed to project out from the top of the cooker;
* pills and medicines are locked away;
* household cleaners and garden chemicals are out of reach;
* there are no small objects lying around which a young child could swallow or push into her nose or ear;
* sharp objects like pencils, scissors and knives are out of the way;
* electric sockets are of the safety type or are properly covered and protected;
* any dangerous windows are securely closed, and not easily opened by determined adventurers;
* there are no plastic bags within reach;
* stair rods and carpets are safe and in good order;
* heavy ornaments are out of reach.

Fire Precautions

The social services department will probably contact the Fire Prevention Officer before a new playgroup, nursery or childminder is registered to make sure that the premises are properly safeguarded. You should make sure that the sort of things s/he recommends are put into practice. Strangely enough, Fire Officers do not automatically go back and check that what they have advised has been properly implemented.

When a Fire Prevention Officer visits a house where children are being cared for s/he is on the lookout for several things. If you have doubts you might make the same checks. There should

★ be a safe way out in case of fire;

★ be adequate fire-fighting equipment, probably a fire extinguisher and a fire blanket at least;

★ be a safe heating system, in particular fires of all kinds should have fixed guards;

★ not be free-standing gas cylinder fires — gas should be piped in from outside;

★ be an acceptable pattern of general housekeeping, in which waste paper is not stacked beside a heater and no-one keeps a can of petrol tucked away in the house.

The officer we spoke to was adamant that, though it seemed unlikely, this sort of thing could happen. 'We get motor-bike-mad teenagers deciding to strip down their machines in their bedrooms,' she explained. 'The results could be horrendous!'

The Quality of Care

Your child needs to feel that she is secure and loved, and she should be encouraged to show her own emotions freely, confident that she will be given a warm response. If she is just learning to talk, understanding and getting to grips with language, then she needs to be talked and read to; she needs to ask questions and know that someone will try to answer them in a way she can understand.

She is also trying to find out about the shapes and feel of things. She will want to draw and scribble, and to build blocks into piles. She will be excited by sound and want the chance to shout and sing, to bang a couple of saucepan lids together, to drum with her spoon on the table. As she gets older and more mobile she will want to run, hop and jump.

Childminders

Bear these needs in mind when you are looking for a childminder, and make absolutely sure that your child will have the chance to play, outside as well as in. You should also be wary of a childminder who keeps the TV on all the time, has no telephone – a vital lifeline in case of emergency – and has nowhere for the children to rest. Many under-fives urgently need to lie down for a mid-morning or afternoon nap. On the other hand, don't trust a minder who wants her charges to stay in bed and snooze or sit still for hours on end. It is also wise to check up on whether your minder has had any previous experience, and whether she will be around for a few years. Children desperately need continuity in their relationships, and it can be very damaging if they learn to love a new mother figure who suddenly moves house and goes out of their life.

Some minders are perfectly happy to take the children in their care along to the local playgroup, and this should be encouraged, but of course it is an extra service for which you should pay extra. In some areas childminders also have access to play centres, toy kits, and toy libraries – and the opportunity to attend courses on child care. Huddersfield's National Children's Centre, for instance, is setting up some fine courses for would-be childminders. Ask your local social services department whether there is such a provision in your neighbourhood. If not, gentle persuasion from people who use childminders, as well as helpful teachers, doctors and so on, may encourage the authorities to take their responsibilities more seriously.

If you need help contact the National Childminding Association (see Directory), which will be glad to advise you. Their stated 'objects and powers' declare that they aim 'to foster and promote the provision of educational, happy, secure and stimulating day-care facilities for young children . . . and to provide help and advice to those looking after other people's children so that the quality of service to children may be improved'.

Remember, though, that the relationship between childminders and the families they serve is a triangular one. Its success depends upon responsible and caring behaviour from the parent as well as from the childminder. If the parent behaves well towards the minder and gets on well with the child, the chances are that the childminder will behave well towards both the parent and the child.

Always treat your childminder with respect and consideration – remember that she may be a working parent, too, with a family of her own to care for, and that she has the same sort of pressures of time and organization that you have. Don't expect her to work miracles or to have time to spend half an hour at the end of an exhausting day discussing your child in detail. If you feel you must have a long talk, make an appointment to see her at a convenient time.

Be prepared to pay a *fair rate* for her care, and agree from the beginning what day is pay day and what charges are payable for absences, sickness and holidays. You should also sort out which of you will provide food – many mothers prefer to organize this themselves. If you want her to take your baby to the clinic she will probably be pleased to do so, but she must be able to prove she has your permission before your child can receive any treatment.

Help your minder help your child to adjust to her care as smoothly as possible. For instance, it might be a good idea for her to take some of her favourite toys and perhaps a special blanket or comforter. The minder should also know about the daily routine she is used to – when she eats, when she sleeps and so on – and about any food fads, allergies or problems.

Suggestions follow for maintaining a good relationship with your childminder:

★ Be sure she has the telephone numbers of both parents at work as well as at home and also of your doctor.

★ Have alternative arrangements in mind in case your minder is ill or otherwise unavailable.

★ Don't take your child to the minder if she is ill, even if it's just a cold.

★ Make sure the child has had all her necessary injections.

★ Don't get behind with your payments on any account. It's just not fair.

★ If you have any worries about the quality of care your child is receiving, discuss it with your minder, but do be tactful and understanding.

★ Let the childminder know if the child will be absent for any reason.

★ Don't be late picking up the child if you can possibly avoid it. If it cannot be avoided, try to ring and let her know.

★ If you can help the minder in any way, do so. You might be able to pick up odd bits of shopping for her, offer her clothes or toys your child doesn't need any longer, take her vegetables from your garden, and so on.

★ Treat her as a friend and equal.

One young couple described to us their successful relationship with their minder: 'If we go away for a day we always bring her a little gift. When we're on holiday we send her a card, and tell her all about it. We always make it clear that we value her enormously, and now she seems like one of the family. She will go out of her way to help us in any way she can, especially in an emergency, and she knows that we will understand if *she* has problems.'

Many parents find a marvellous childminder who loves and cares for their baby almost as much as they do. However, if something goes wrong and you begin to feel anxious for some reason, you shouldn't just ignore it and hope that things will sort themselves out. Your first step should be to talk to your minder as tactfully and sympathetically as possible. If this doesn't work, go to the social services department, ask to see the Childminding Adviser, and put your problem to her. If the worst comes to the worst you may have to move your child to another minder, but try to avoid this if you possibly can. Consistent care is important.

Babysitters

Though a babysitter may not play as large a part in a child's life as a childminder, she can nevertheless be an important person in the child's world and should be chosen with the same care. Once found, she should be treated with consideration so that the relationship will be a long and happy one.

We have dealt already (in Chapter Two) with choosing a suitable babysitter. But there are other practical problems. A child may cry for hours when you have left her and the babysitter, so as not to worry you, may not mention it. Such distress, if it recurs consistently, can have a serious effect on the child's development. It may be that she feels insecure – if so, you should try very hard to build up her security with a lot of attention and loving care. And you should always, no matter how hurried you are, make sure to prepare her to be without you for a little while.

If she is likely to be asleep throughout the sit it is still advisable that she should meet the sitter in advance. It can be a terrible shock for a child to be confronted by a stranger if she wakes in the middle of the night. However, with agency sitters this is not always possible, and some children become so accustomed to different sitters that they are unperturbed. Nonetheless, the child must be told that a sitter is going to be there if she is old enough to understand.

If there is a chance – and there usually is – of the child needing the sitter in the course of the evening, then they really *should* meet in advance, if only by the sitter coming half an hour early. Make sure the sitter and your child know each other's names, especially if one is unusual or the sitter is not used to the English language.

Try to go through bedtime rituals in exactly the same way as usual. Give the child her bath without rushing her, let her have her normal play and her usual bedtime story without hurrying or stinting your attention. However, if you play or fuss with her more than usual she may either get too excited or very suspicious, and refuse to sleep.

If your child will be up for a while after you leave then make certain the sitter comes early enough so that you can be with them both for a time before you have to leave. Tell the sitter anything she may need to know in a calm, unhurried way. If you rush around frantically showing where everything is, your anxiety will communicate itself to the child and she'll be upset. And when you go, *don't* make a performance of it or she may think she's going to be abandoned for ever. If she does cry when you leave, don't keep coming back again and again to soothe her. She'll just cry more and more every time you leave again. Either play with her for a quarter of an hour or so or go.

On the other hand, don't disappear suddenly without letting her know you're going – the sudden realization that you are gone will cause ructions. Don't lie, either. It's not a good idea to say you'll be back in five minutes. When it becomes obvious that you're not coming back she will feel betrayed, and next time you need a babysitter the child will feel so insecure she'll make life impossible for both of you and your evening will be ruined. It is amazing how many parents do this, trapped by a child's tears into lying even though they know it is counter-productive.

Make sure that the babysitter has all the information she could possibly need before you go out, and that all possible preparations have been made. Leave her a list of telephone numbers including those of your doctor, a friend – preferably a neighbour – and, if possible, the place you will be. If a potty will be needed, show the sitter where it is and tell her at what time the child usually uses it and if she will need reminding or help. If a nappy will have to be changed, leave out a clean nappy, a nappy bin, cream, tissues and a hand towel, and tell her where and how you usually change it.

Tell the sitter whether your child is accustomed to having her light left on or if she is to have anything special to eat or drink if she wakes. Explain your method of dealing with crying – some children fall asleep again more easily if they are attended to immediately they cry, others are best left alone for half a minute or so to stop crying of their own accord.

Obviously to spank or not to spank is one of the details that must be agreed between sitter and parent from the beginning, but this is not necessarily an easy question to answer. A young child is often able to take in her stride a slap from a parent because she knows that, despite everything, she is loved. But the same slap from an angry stranger may be a very different and frightening experience that might trigger off all manner of traumas. Our view is that smacking should be avoided if at all possible – though gently firm insistence on doing the right thing should be encouraged. A babysitter who allows a child to go to bed without cleaning her teeth, to stay up to watch a television programme her parents usually forbid, or to stuff herself on sweets that are normally rationed, is not doing the job properly. But remember that nobody, with the possible exception of the child, ever really knows what goes on once the parents leave.

Yet it is often assumed that the babysitter's job is an easy one and that the pay is more than adequate. In fact, babysitters have to put up with awkward hours and virtual imprisonment in your house. There is no regularity about their income and they must accept a great deal of responsibility. They have the nail-biting strain of looking after children without the pleasure of them being their own; they can be bored or tense, confined in a stranger's home for hours on end without company; and they can't even relax into a late-night television show confident that they will be able to see the end.

If they are taken for granted they may become unavailable when you ask for their help, but if treated well they could become the very backbone of all your free evenings. The following list of suggestions may seem obvious to parents who already treat their sitters well, but common courtesy is surprisingly easy to forget.

★ Don't pretend you'll be back early if you know you're going to be late.
★ Always leave some sort of meal – if only some bread and cheese. The cost is negligible when spread over a few hours'

sitting, and those who only leave a couple of teabags will soon be let down.

★ You will get a better service if you pay the full going rate. The moment of payment is usually embarrassing and those who take advantage of this by only paying a four-hour fee for what has, in fact, been four hours and ten minutes will often find that the babysitter is not free when next they call her. She has made it possible for you to have an evening out, and you have given her meanness in return.

★ If she wants to sit for other people, encourage her to use you as a reference once you know her well enough and pass her name on to your friends. You may occasionally find her booked and unavailable when you need her, but it's worth it in the long run. She might, for example, rearrange her own nights out to fit in with yours as a way of thanking you.

★ Book her as much in advance as possible to allow her a certain amount of security. But *never* hesitate to call her, even at the very last minute – she will never mind being asked if your place is the most agreeable on her list.

★ When you really have no preference as to which of two evenings you want to go out, ask her which *she* would prefer.

★ Don't ring her early in the morning, as she may have been sitting for someone else very late the night before.

★ Find out from her the best times to ring, for if you constantly miss her you'll both lose the regularity you want.

★ If the sitter is a student, leave a desk or table clear for her to work at; the more productively she feels the time is spent, the more she'll be willing to come back.

★ If, when you return, she's in the middle of a television programme, pay her what you owe her and ask if she would like to stay and watch it to the end (if it makes no difference to you). Or ask her to stay and have coffee with you. Remember, it can be boring being a babysitter – if friendships develop the job seems much more worthwhile.

★ If you cancel a booking – and this happens to babysitters one time out of four – offer her half of what you would have paid her and more if you have not given her any notice. After all, you won't have spent what you would if you'd gone out. The sitter has probably relied on the money and maybe even the meal, and she may have turned down other bookings because of yours.

Daytime babysitters are obviously required to do much more for the children in their charge than those who are able to put them to bed and relax. Consider whether the extra responsibility and work deserve extra payment. Certainly you should be even more careful about making sure that they get on well with the children and are prepared to play with them and keep them happily occupied.

Daytime babysitting may prove an ideal job for an energetic pensioner, and in our experience older people often manage amazingly successfully with children. They have time to give them their full attention and they have a fund of experience and often a lot of good stories and games tucked away in their long memories. They relish the company of youngsters, since they may feel deprived of it. Our society too often segregates itself by age and the elderly find that they spend all their time with other elderly people, which can be boring and disheartening. An hour or two every now and then with a lively toddler can, quite literally, give them a new lease of life, and the friendship that may develop with you and the rest of your family is an added bonus. In our opinion every young family needs grandparents, whether they are related or not. But do remember that they will not have the same reserves of energy as younger people, so if your children are wildly active and demanding, consider that older people may find them too exhausting. We heard of one three-year-old boy who managed to lock his babysitter and little sister out in the back garden, from which there was no escape, and then spent the next three-and-a-half hours industriously decorating the gold-leafed walls and expensive inlaid furniture with purple crayon. And the helpless sitter had to watch him through the glass doors!

Actors are frequently out of work or free during the day while performing at night. Some middle-aged housewives whose own children have left home are glad to fill the gap in their lives with other people's children, and obviously experience has made them very competent. And many unemployed but nevertheless very capable young people are keen to earn a little money. Vet them carefully, though, and *do* get a reference. Those who have younger brothers or sisters, have a lot of experience in evening babysitting, or who are looking for a job in child care may be the safest bets.

Pop into your local careers office, which specializes in finding work for the young. They tend to know the teenagers on their books very well if they are doing their job properly. There may be some who have completed a Youth Opportunities Programme but still haven't found work and desperately need something to keep them occupied, for the sake of their morale and self-respect as much as their pocket.

Choose your babysitter carefully and then follow through by treating her with kindness and consideration. You and your children may have found a friend for life.

5
HOLIDAYS AND HOLIDAY CARE

It isn't until school holidays come round – especially the long, long, summer holiday – that parents really begin to appreciate school teachers! The fact is, children need a lot of organizing and supervising, even when they are well into their teens. It's not just a matter of keeping them safe and fed – there's also the complicated business of keeping them happily occupied. Every parent knows that sinking of the heart when their child looks at them in grim despair and wails 'What can I do?'

The Student

Probably the simplest arrangement is to find a student, either from this country or abroad, who is looking for a holiday job which she can do either on a daily or residential basis. You can find such a student in several ways. You could advertise in a national paper for a residential help, though a local paper might be more useful for a daily help. Or you could put an advertisement on the notice board of your nearest college or university. You could advertise in the excellent annual book *Summer Jobs in Britain* published by Vacation Work (see Directory), or in one of its two supplements published in May and June. (But remember to give them adequate time before they go to press.) Or you could use one of the agencies listed in the book – most of these specialize in short-stay help. Or you could answer one of the many advertisements put into the newspapers by students looking for holiday work. The possibilities are endless. Do remember, though, that students are people, too. They won't put up with being overworked, underpaid, or unjustly treated by an exploitative employer any more than you would. But they will, as a rule, respond very willingly to fair and friendly treatment.

But this problem has now reached such massive proportions – especially since so many school-age children come from families where both parents are employed – that many organizations are working very hard to provide holiday playschemes and projects which go some way, at least, towards easing the difficulties.

Playschemes

No two playschemes are exactly the same. They vary from place to place depending upon the leader, the children, the neighbourhood and the facilities they have at their disposal. Some run all summer, some only last for a week or two. Some cater for all children, some are limited to children with particular social needs or a specific handicap. Some are for children of a narrow age group.

Basically, though, playschemes are periods of daily play for school-age children, supervised by at least one trained play-leader and several voluntary assistants. The activities organized may include adventure play, games, sport, outings and visits, arts and crafts, drama and hobbies.

Several local authorities run their own playschemes. To find out if yours does, contact the social services department and/or the local education authority, or ask at the Citizens' Advice Bureau.

If you feel very strongly that your child *particularly* needs to join in a local playscheme – either because you cannot provide for her adequately at home or because of trouble in the family, or because she herself needs the social contact – ask a social worker or the child's headteacher to put forward her name to the playscheme organizer with a request that she should be given priority. Normally a small charge is made for places, but in cases of financial difficulty this may be waived. Some holiday playschemes are especially for handicapped children or will take handicapped children (see Chapter Six).

A centre of information for summer holiday playschemes is the National Playing Fields Association (see Directory), which produces an excellent comprehensive *Play and Volunteer Directory*. It contains a register of playschemes including those for handicapped children. The association has what is probably the largest collection of books, reports, pamphlets, surveys, photographs, slides and films on children's play and recreation in the UK. Most of these can be borrowed, and of course all their own publications can be bought. They also have an up-to-date list of organizations involved in play and recreation as well as details of conferences and workshops both in this country and abroad.

Because the local authority provision of holiday care is not sufficient to meet the need, it is augmented by a great deal of independent effort, coordinated by national organizations such as Gingerbread, the National Playbus Association, the London Adventure Playground Association (which gives advice nationally), the British Association for Settlements and Social Action Centres, and Dr Barnardo's. In addition, practically every area has small-scale voluntary groups.

Some local radio stations run effective telephone services – London's Capital 'Kidsline' gives information about holiday playschemes, things to do and places to visit. Other local stations could be encouraged to do the same (it's 'good copy'). Capital has also started keeping a contact register so that parents who phone in from the same district can be put in touch with each other for mutual holiday self-help. The purpose of local radio is to be the mouthpiece of the local community, and this is one way that it can speak on their behalf.

If there is no holiday playscheme in your area but you know that the need is there, it might be a good idea to get together a group of interested parents and see if you can get one off the ground. An advertisement or letter in the local paper or a few postcards in nearby shop windows would probably be enough to form a group, and it could grow from there.

A great deal of information is available on setting-up and running holiday playschemes. The National Playing Fields Association publishes two pamphlets, and several books have been published on organized play (see Booklist).

Residential Holidays

The holiday playschemes described so far are all day schemes, but of course there are many residential holidays for children in this country and abroad, provided that you can afford it *and* that the child is happy to go away from home without you and to muck in with other children.

It is not wise to despatch a child on holiday unless the organization involved has been well recommended by someone whose judgement you trust *or* you have taken pains to visit and investigate the holiday centre yourself. In this field – as in most others – there are one or two unscrupulous operators.

Such holidays should not be seen as a means of getting rid of children. Unaccompanied holidays should be thoroughly good experiences for everyone – as well as being a relief for parents – and should be carefully considered beforehand. The cost varies considerably, but their growing popularity shows that most are within the average parent's budget.

Particularly recommended are Colony Holidays for eight-to fifteen-year-olds, with their special mixture of adventure, culture and crafts (see Directory). This organization has proved itself so valuable that occasionally local authorities are prepared to contribute towards the costs of children who would benefit from one of their holidays but whose parents cannot afford the fee.

PGL Young Adventure Ltd (see Directory) is one of the largest children's holiday organizers, one of its centres covering 248 acres and a farm in Shropshire. They cater for seven- to seventeen-year-olds, keeping the age groups separate, and have experienced staff. The Youth Hostels Association (see Directory) also offers a wide range of adventure holidays to youngsters from eleven to sixteen, but they do have a distressingly chauvinistic tendency to exclude girls from such activities as fishing, mountain adventure and wildlife safaris.

The YMCA National Centre in Southampton offers children of ten to seventeen, as individuals or in groups, one- or two-week holidays involving archery, canoeing, orienteering, riding and sailing. They are supervised by trained professional youth workers and instructors, and all equipment is provided. Their professed aim is 'to develop an appreciation of nature, to learn tolerance, self-reliance and the ability to get on with other people through living, working and playing together in small groups under a leader, and to learn the application of Christian values to everyday living'.

Outward Bound (see Directory) has five centres in the mountains and by the sea and is another holiday venture which combines exciting activities with stimulating social experience. It runs seven-day Preliminary Courses for ten- to thirteen-year-olds, two- or three-week Junior Courses for fourteen- to sixteen-year-olds, and three-week Standard Courses for sixteen- to twenty-year-olds. Again, all equipment is provided free, and instruction is by experts.

Discovery Holidays of Northern Ireland (see Directory) is non-denominational and aims to give children between eight and fifteen throughout Ulster a much-needed break. School buildings are transformed into summer hostels, activities cover a very wide range, and staff are trained and experienced. This is a charitable organization and charges between a quarter and a third of the parent's weekly wage, subsidizing the rest.

Details of a huge range of other adventure/activity holidays can be gathered from the books and pamphlets listed in the Booklist. *Adventure Holidays*, published by VacWork, is very comprehensive and deals with holidays for children from five upwards. It is available from most big bookshops or Vacation Work Publications. *Children on Holiday*, published by the British Tourist Authority, covers children from six to sixteen. *Sports and Adventure Holidays*, published by the Central Bureau, caters for children of about twelve upwards and gives details of sporting and cultural visits to fifty-four countries including Britain, with advice on fares, insurance, medical requirements, and so on. Some of the holidays sound immensely exciting – coral diving in the Red Sea, for example – but naturally the more ambitious tend to be the more expensive. It includes a directory of all the main children's holiday centres and gives guidance on them. *Adventure Holidays* is published by the Youth Hostels Association, free of charge. It contains details of eighty holidays for eleven- to sixteen-year-olds and gives some indication of the degree of difficulty of the activity involved. Some of the holidays are for boys and girls, others are single-sex.

Many social organizations and churches organize children's holidays, too – but usually only for those who have been involved with their activities throughout the year. If your child has been involved with the Scouts or Guides, a Youth Club or a Boys or Girls Brigade, or is an active member of a youth group attached to a religious organization, it is very likely that s/he will have the opportunity to go away with them. This sort of holiday has several advantages, in that the children are often with friends so loneliness or homesickness are not major problems.

These holidays are usually organized with volunteer help and are often very simple – accommodation may be under canvas or in spartan youth hostels, and food may be pretty basic – so it should not cost as much as if it were set up by a professional holiday agency. Don't worry if the provision seems a bit primitive and not what your family is used to: children *thrive* on the simple life and find it an adventure to wash under an outside tap or drink their bedtime cocoa out of the same mug they've just used for their soup.

Some schools also organize holidays. They may not be of much help to parents needing holiday care if they are educational cruises or foreign visits that may only take place in term time, but if they are timed to coincide with the holidays they can be a boon. Many are projects of some sort – perhaps the children go fruit-picking at a harvest camp, visit a farm, go to a field-study centre, or get involved in some sporting activity such as climbing, canoeing, sailing or orienteering. Holidays of this sort are packed with excitement and adventure and the children are rarely bored. They are exposed to all sorts of new experiences and learn to live in a group, to share and give and take, and to get along even with people they do not like. In short, they are an extremely valuable part of growing up and are truly 'educational' in the best sense of the word.

Exchange Holidays

Another sort of educational holiday experience is the foreign exchange. In this system your child spends a holiday with a family abroad, and then that family sends their child back to you for a holiday in Britain. This may all happen in the long summer holiday, or it may be spread over a year or so; perhaps a French child will spend an English summer by the seaside and an English child visit the French countryside at Easter.

The various agencies which arrange foreign exchanges say that children from nine upwards can fit in happily with this sort of holiday, although it seems to us that a nine-year-old may not be sufficiently self-assured to adapt to an unknown foreign family and cope with the language difficulties. For younger children it may be a better idea to send two together – either two school friends or two children from the same family – to a foreign family who would like to send two of their children back to you. For a child on her own the ideal age to begin is about twelve or thirteen, and these first visits often result in return visits over several years.

There are various ways of finding host families. Perhaps you have your own personal contacts abroad who may be able to put you in touch with suitable friends. Or you can develop contacts through your children's pen-friends found either through the school or through the Central Bureau for Educational Visits and Exchanges (see Directory), which will help free of charge to provide pen-friends in France, Germany, Italy, Spain, the USSR and many other countries for school pupils aged ten to eighteen. They will also arrange pen-friends for whole classes.

Once a pen-pal friendship is built up an exchange visit can work very well, since the children who have busily written to each other will have exchanged news, family details and photographs and will feel, before they even meet, that they already know each other well.

Another way of forging links is through the 'Twinning' scheme. Many towns and villages in the UK are twinned with towns or villages in other countries; many people do not realize that their town is linked with four or five others. If yours is one, your local council will be able to tell you more about it and give you information about organizations to contact for finding a suitable exchange family. The Joint Twinning Committee of the Local Authorities Association of Great Britain (see Directory) publishes a booklet called *Places in Partnership* which lists about a thousand twinnings (see Booklist).

However, most foreign exchanges are organized either through the school – usually with the help of the Central

Bureau – or through a commercial agency. The work of the Central Bureau, along with a mass of useful addresses and detailed information and advice, is outlined in an invaluable booklet called *School Travel and Exchange* (see Booklist), published annually and available from them.

Of the various holiday agencies operating in this field Robertson's Educational Travel Service (see Directory), with over thirty years' experience, is a respected example. It specializes in German, Spanish and French links and takes great care to match families as well as individual children as far as interests and background are concerned. Of course you, as a parent, should be particularly careful to make sure that some real common interest exists between your child and the host child. It is probably a recipe for disaster to send a rough, extrovert rugby fanatic to spend a fortnight with a youth who hates sport but adores poetry or the theatre!

This matching of interests is much more important than the geographical area in which the host family lives, so be prepared to be flexible about geography. On the other hand, it may not be your child's idea of fun to spend a long, hot summer stuck in the industrial heart of a big city, no matter how charming her host family, so consider carefully before you commit yourself.

Families usually take great care of your child and treat her very kindly, if only because their son or daughter will soon be dependent upon *you* for kindness and generosity. It is very much a case of 'do as you would be done by'.

Dates of school holidays abroad are sometimes different from those in this country, but usually schools are willing either to allow a few days off at the end of term or to make the visiting child welcome at school.

Of course, the fact that you send your child away for an educational exchange so that someone else will be looking after her for a chunk of the school holidays also means that you will have to spend time looking after someone else's child at some later stage. Unless you can positively commit yourself to this and know that you can make a foreign child welcome and entertain her properly, it is not the right system for you.

However, an inability to do this need not necessarily exclude

71

your child from an educational foreign holiday. Some agencies can arrange foreign *guest* visits to countries abroad, and the Central Bureau has many suggestions for cheap accommodation, summer camps, courses and study schools. The fact remains that exchanges are much *cheaper*, and if a visit from a foreign child can be fitted in with your own summer holiday it may be that much more fun for the family.

Incidentally, there's no reason why the pen-pal exchange idea should be limited to exchanges between different countries. A UK city child and another from a farm or country village, for instance, could probably learn as much from getting to know and visit each other as one from Frankfurt and one from Birmingham. The easiest way to organize this yourself is to put a small ad in a magazine or national newspaper and see what develops – but do take care to find out enough about the host family to make sure that your child has a good chance of fitting in there. It would be a good idea to work out a few questions to ask applicants, along the lines of the following:

★ What are your child's main interests?
★ What sort of holiday do you plan for the children when they are with you?
★ What sort of holiday activities would you like for your child when she is staying with us?
★ What are your own occupations and interests?
★ How many are there in the family and what are the ages of the other children?
★ In what sort of district is your house/flat situated?
★ What sort of sleeping accommodation will you provide for our child?

6
THE HANDICAPPED CHILD

It is harder to find people to look after a home-based handicapped child than it is to obtain child care for her more fortunate sister. And yet it is more necessary, for three reasons. To start with, a child with a mental or physical handicap is more in need of a variety of experiences, relationships and places so that her life has some of the richness and stimuli automatically available to other children.

Equally importantly, handicapped children, no matter how loved they are, do tend to exhaust their parents physically, mentally and emotionally, and often only by being separated from time to time can adults regain some of the energy and stamina they need to care for their children properly.

And inevitably there are times when it is almost impossible for parents to take their child with them: visits to the doctor or a hospital, or supermarket shopping, can become hazards with a handicapped child in tow. However, if the parent *can* manage to take the child along there is the advantage that she will become more accepted locally.

Babysitting

Babysitters may be quite happy to look after a handicapped child provided the handicap is reasonably easy to cope with, but they *must always* be fully informed. It is quite unfair of parents to arrange care for a handicapped child without explaining that she *is* handicapped, and what the handicap is. As for children with a very severe handicap, there are still people around who are prepared to look after them. The best plan is for the potential sitter to spend some time with the family beforehand to see what exactly is involved – whether the child has to be fed or undressed, for instance, or taken to the lavatory, or lifted and carried. If the child responds to her without feeling upset, and if the sitter feels at ease and confident that she can cope, then the parent can leave them

73

together without worrying.

If all you need is simple babysitting, but are unable to find it, look into some of the excellent babysitting schemes already in operation. For instance, in Bristol local medical students make a regular commitment to look after handicapped children, free of charge, either at home or on weekend holidays. Such a system could be set up elsewhere.

Some social services departments run 'Good Neighbour' schemes in which people offer help and support and often volunteer to babysit during the day. Most towns also have Councils of Voluntary Service which bring together volunteers who want to assist people who need help. Requests for help are usually passed on by doctors or social workers.

Another idea is to advertise, either in a shop window or in your local paper, describing exactly what sort of care you require. Or you could write a letter to your paper, explaining your difficulty and asking for advice and help from anyone who may be able to lend a hand. You may find that other parents in a similar dilemma will get in touch with you or write to the paper, which could be the beginning of a self-help group for parents of handicapped children who could perhaps babysit for each other. The newspaper may well feel sufficiently involved to launch a publicity campaign on your behalf. Alternatively, your letter may provoke a response from organizations in the area which are able to help. There are usually many of these, including the Water Rats, Rotary Club, Round Table, Trades Council, Lions, Chamber of Commerce, Women's Institute, and National Council of Women. All provide voluntary help of some sort to people in need.

Young people also volunteer for community service. It may be that senior pupils at your local secondary school or sixth-form college, or students from the nearest polytechnic, college of further education or university, will offer their services. And often those working for the Duke of Edinburgh award are looking for a community project of this sort in which to get involved.

Another way to find useful organizations is to go along to the local Citizens' Advice Bureau or social services department and ask if they can advise you. You could also get hold of a copy of *Voluntary Social Services* from the National Council for Voluntary Organizations (see Directory). This is a directory of national organizations of all kinds. Or you could get in touch with the national headquarters of some of the voluntary organizations which exist specifically to help the handicapped, and see if they know of any body of people in your area which would be prepared to help.

The best known of these organizations as far as mental handicap is concerned are MIND and the National Society for Mentally Handicapped Children (see Directory). The latter produces an excellent, helpful and morale-boosting monthly magazine called *Parents' Voice*. It was also responsible for establishing the Gateway Clubs which organize leisure and social activities for the mentally handicapped. Most clubs can offer a wide range of sports as well as arts and crafts. And they may encourage their members to learn new skills to help themselves, *and* to involve themselves in activities to help others in the community. For instance, they may do gardening or work on reclaiming land for a children's playground. The feeling that they are useful and productive members of society can be a very valuable boost to their self-esteem.

For physically handicapped children there is the Invalid Children's Aid Association and PHAB (Physically Handicapped/Able Bodied) (see Directory) as well as a great many particularly involved with a specific type of disability, such as the Down's Children's Association or the British Epilepsy Association.

But perhaps the best source of information to start out with is the Voluntary Council for Handicapped Children (see Directory), which provides a booklet called *Help Starts Here*, specifically designed to explain to parents of children with special needs how they can find out about the help available. It is available free of charge from the council.

Playgroups

For more regular or comprehensive child care you may find that there is a pre-school playgroup for handicapped children near where you live. Some of these are run by the National Society for Mentally Handicapped Children, Dr Barnardo's or the Invalid Children's Aid Association. The Pre-school Playgroups Association also encourages member groups to provide for handicapped children, as well as having some groups for handicapped children only. The association produces literature about handicapped children and playgroups, which you can obtain from them by writing to their head office (see Directory). It also has a national adviser with responsibility for special needs who can give information on any aspect of this topic.

Now part of the Pre-school Playgroups Association are Opportunity Groups, playgroups where children with any form of handicap can play together with 'normal' children and where their mothers can get to know each other. Opportunity Groups are open to children from birth so that the important business of learning and developing through play can begin as soon as possible. The ideal number is twenty children in all, with a maximum of thirteen being handicapped in some way. *Notes for Opportunity Groups* by Dr R. E. Faulkner, who first founded them, is available from the association. The philosophy behind the organization of Opportunity Groups is very much in line with contemporary trends which aim to *integrate* the handicapped child into society as a whole rather than segregate her. This has been found to be of benefit not only to the handicapped but also to the able-bodied with whom they come into contact. Certainly handicap, either physical or mental, can hardly be considered a rare thing – about one in thirty of us is handicapped in some way. It is very much to the advantage of our society if *all* of us – not just a few specialist teachers, social workers, medical personnel, and volunteers – learn to come to terms with this, rid ourselves of fears or inhibitions, and accept it as part of life.

Day Centres

As well as the benefits provided by occasional or regular babysitting and playgroup sessions, parents of handicapped children may find that day centres are a great help both to them and their child. In fact, these may be the factor that decides whether the child can stay at home with her parents or has to be institutionalized in a hospital.

In some areas social services departments face up to the responsibility of providing day care. In others it is left to a hospital or a voluntary society like Dr Barnardo's, the National Children's Home, or the Spastics Society (see Directory). However, the social services department should at least know about what is available locally even if it is not involved. Very often handicapped centres spring into being through the coordinated and continuous pressure and lobbying of a strong local group. If you feel that you could work towards such a venture in your own area, take courage from the fact that other groups have fought this battle and *won*.

For instance, the Hornsey Handicapped Children's Centre was built and maintained by a trust. It now provides:

★ nursery school facilities;

★ supervision for children so that parents can have a few hours to themselves;

★ a therapy centre;

★ an evening social club for mentally handicapped children and young people; and

★ a recreational centre for handicapped children and their parents.

In Exeter the National Health Service organizes an excellent family support and treatment unit for young handicapped children living at home. Among the many facilities it provides is care for infants from periods ranging from one day at a time to a fortnight, so that their parents can have a break.

These two schemes are outlined in a survey called *Spotlight on Services for the Young Handicapped Child* by Jessie Parfitt (see Booklist). Much of the information is very valuable ammunition for persuading either the National Health Service or the social services department that they should be doing more to help this particular section of the community, which needs all the help it can get. There are several parents' groups working in the UK, but for the most part their activities are local. However, a group called Kith and Kids has not only done imaginative pioneering work and established itself as a formidable and respected pressure group, but in 1976 it also produced a book, *Kith and Kids: Self-Help for Families of the Handicapped* by Maurice and Doreen Collins (see Booklist), which is of great value to other parents trying to help their children and themselves by community action.

Playschemes

Rather easier to find than comprehensive day-care centres are playschemes and holiday opportunities for the handicapped. Sometimes handicapped children have their own adventure playgrounds especially geared to their needs, but these are usually connected to particular hospitals or schools purely for the use of their own children, so no comprehensive list is available. Nevertheless, if you have a handicapped child and know of a nearby handicapped playground from which she is excluded because she is home-based rather than residential, *do* ask if she can use it. Just as there is a move to persuade the authorities to free the facilities of schools for use by the whole community, so there should be a move to persuade handicapped schools or hospitals to welcome a little integration with the world outside their walls – self-help groups supported and advised by full-time professional staff.

A society called the Handicapped Adventure Playground Association runs playgrounds of its own and is associated with others which share a similar philosophy, staffing quotient, and so on, but as yet these are few and far between. More are urgently needed. The association (see Directory) will provide you with a list of playgrounds.

Perhaps the most useful organization is the National Playing Fields Association (see Directory), which is particularly concerned about the play and leisure needs of handicapped children. It can give information and advice and in some cases a little bit of financial assistance. It also has regional advisers who can give local advice, and it produces several pamphlets on various aspects of play for the handicapped. Especially valuable is their annual *Play and Volunteer Directory*, which lists, county by county, various holiday playschemes including those specifically designed for or designed to include handicapped children.

Unfortunately, even today, a certain amount of stupid, ignorant prejudice exists against handicapped people, especially those who are mentally handicapped. Usually the prejudice stems from fear, but that doesn't make it any easier to cope with. If you find that difficulties are being made about your child being allowed to join in a local playscheme, and if it seems that those difficulties are based on prejudice rather than genuine reasons, don't just give in. Get in touch with the Fair Play For Children campaign (see Directory), which may be prepared to intervene. The argument may not have been considered that instead of 'normal' children losing out on a supervisor's attention when a handicapped child is present, all the children could gain a great deal from the presence of a child who needs a little consideration.

Unaccompanied Holidays

Unaccompanied holidays for handicapped children should fulfil two requirements. They should give parents a much-needed rest and – very important – they should give the children some fun, extend their horizons and develop their skills and experiences. So try to choose a holiday with care.

Some of the bigger voluntary societies – the National Society for Mentally Handicapped Children, Toc H, Save The Children, Dr Barnardo's, the Shaftesbury Society, the Lady Hoare Trust for Physically Disabled Children and the British Red Cross Society (see Directory) – run their own holiday schemes. Many religious bodies do so as well. PHAB clubs do excellent work in bringing together physically-handicapped and able-bodied people on residential courses where they can work together on art, music, drama, outdoor activities and sports, and there are many other organizations which either arrange special holidays or welcome handicapped children into their regular holiday schemes. Enquiries to organizations dealing with your child's specific handicap, or from local county or town welfare departments, may tell you of those nearest you.

Don't be put off trying to provide your child with a holiday away from home because of the cost. Social services departments may be able to arrange or advise about inexpensive holidays. Sometimes they cooperate with the voluntary organizations, sometimes they find funds to subsidize the cost of a holiday you arrange yourself. Or you could contact the Education Welfare Officer of your local education authority or one of her School Care Workers to see if they can help in any way. The Royal Association for Disability and Rehabilitation (see Directory) runs a holiday information service for physically handicapped people and publishes an annual guidebook, *Holidays for the Physically Handicapped,* which lists both private accommodation and voluntary organizations offering holidays. It should be available at bookshops.

The excellent *Handbook for Parents with a Handicapped Child* by Judith Stone and Felicity Taylor, published in 1977 (see Booklist), is an extraordinarily useful source of information on all aspects of handicap. It has a very good chapter on holidays as well as some valuable suggestions about residential special-interest and sports courses such as those offered by the Outward Bound Trust (see Directory) in a cheering chapter called 'Fun and Friends'.

In all the solemn talk about looking after handicapped children there is one aspect that is often overlooked – for them, whether their handicap is physical or mental, life can be *fun*. Many get great joy from the simple processes of daily living. It is up to everybody to try to give them the framework within which that happiness can develop and be sustained, while at the same time making sure that their parents also have their share of comfort and support.

7

DO YOU REALLY NEED A BABYSITTER?

Formal, organized babysitting is a comparatively new phenomenon. Fifty years ago babysitters didn't exist. Families who could afford it employed staff to look after their children – other people coped on their own. And cope they did, rearing the children within a warm, interlocking and secure group of familiar faces that had the added advantage of making the other members of the family, married or single, old or young, employed, out of work or retired, feel wanted and useful, too. Now, in most places, the extended family has split up and scattered and will probably never again be part of our lifestyle. Grandparents may not see their grandchildren for years on end, cousins remain strangers to each other, uncles and nieces may never meet.

Use Your Own Family Group

If you are lucky enough to remain relatively close to your family, you would be wise to cultivate their friendship and support – ditch your differences, get over your grievances, and clutch them to your bosom. They will make splendid babysitters and childminders. They will love your children and your children will love *them*, even though occasionally they may get on your nerves. Of course, some families always get on splendidly together with never a cross word – if you belong to one of them you're lucky. But if you're not you'll be amazed to find how children can strengthen family ties that have loosened.

Create A New Family Group

Sadly the extended family is no longer available as a babysitting solution for many of us. But it is possible to create your own family of friends and neighbours if you work at it. In many streets or blocks of flats there are older people who are happy to have some contact with a young family – a middle-aged woman whose own children have left home leaving her with time and love to spare; a retired couple who rarely see their own grandchildren; a single man or woman who would dearly love to relate to a family. Needless to say, it is not fair to expect these people to look after your children while you give nothing back, but there may be things you can do for them which would make an acceptable swap.

Take A Lodger

Another solution to the problem, if you have room, is to have a lodger. If your children are old enough to manage to some extent on their own then the mere presence of an adult in the house may give you many opportunities to get out – if you have chosen a suitable lodger. It may be worth renting the accommodation at a much reduced price in order to attract such a person, for this arrangement can work extremely well. Often the lodger becomes one of the family and a long-term friend.

If you want to rely on the lodger for specific help you must start properly, on a sound, agreed basis, preferably in writing, so that everyone knows exactly what is expected of them. For instance, make clear how many hours' babysitting you are asking for – if its cash value is more than the accommodation is worth, you may have to pay extra. If it is less than the accommodation could attract, then the lodger could either be asked to pay you some rent or to help in some other way. You should also work out in advance whether the actual sitting should be during the day, in the evenings or both; how much notice you'll give each time or if you are to have a regular timetable; whether you will guarantee not to ask for babysitting on some evenings in the week. Otherwise she's going to find it very difficult to organize her own work and social life. Also agree how much notice either you or she will give if one of you wants to bring the arrangement to an end.

You and she may prefer to be very easygoing about arrangements – perhaps the best way for the system to work – but several important issues must be considered and agreed upon first, so don't rush into a scheme like this without thinking it through carefully. If you find the right person and the right formula, you could find it makes life much, much easier. So much so, in fact, that we would strongly recommend anyone who expects to need a lot of babysitting to carefully consider this if and when they are able to buy a house. It pays dividends to find a place with an extra room or rooms which can be turned into a bed-sitting room or flatlet, if you can afford it. The possibility of having someone else living under your roof can bring you freedom and save you money – or even make you money – very effectively. If you live in a council house or other rented accommodation you'll need to check that you are allowed to take a tenant beforehand.

Your lodger may stay for years or just a few months, but once you've established the system it should not be difficult to find replacements – you might go on having students from the same college, for instance. But if you use this system to help you manage a full-time job then you will need another fall-back possibility. The girl cannot always be expected to arrange her holidays, exams or illnesses to a schedule. However, a large number of sensible students will be happy with this set-up and with a little consideration from you it may be ideal both economically and socially.

Yet another possibility is to advertise for the services of a part-time au pair. She would be expected to do only a certain amount of babysitting or housework in return for, say, a rent-free room. No money or meals need be given, or very little. However, considering the cost of living, it would probably be necessary for her to have another source of income.

Share A House

There are other ways of acquiring home-based help. For instance, we know two families who had been friends for years who bought a large house together and divided it into two flats. Each family has its own, individual way of life and its privacy, but nearly always at least one adult is at home to look after all the children if necessary. This arrangement can easily be adapted to other situations – two adjoining semis, for instance, preferably with a linking inside door, or adjacent flats in a large block.

Success or failure depends very much on the behaviour of

those taking part. For instance, if one family needs babysitting much more than the other, or if one child is much more difficult to look after, problems can arise. There are various ways of coping with this sort of imbalance. For instance, the family with the greater need can supplement the child care provided by the other family by bringing in outside babysitters from time to time. Or it can return its obligations in other ways – by helping out with shopping, washing, gardening or whatever is needed. Or it can provide an occasional treat, like a family feast, or a day out, or a trip to the cinema – whatever would be most enjoyed by the overworked babysitters.

Again and again while researching this book we discovered that those who found it easiest to organize care of any sort for their children were those who made a continuous effort to be considerate and generous towards their helpers. Frequently the quality of care the children receive depends entirely on the relationship between the adults concerned. This may seem grossly unfair, but if you treat your helpers badly your children may suffer in the long run.

Try Communal Living

A further development of the idea of living in adjacent or communicating flats or houses with friends and helping each other with all your children is communal living. The idea of living in a commune or community terrifies most people. They feel that their privacy, independence and individuality will be threatened and dread the thought of having to use communal facilities, share a kitchen and laundry, and so on. In fact, no two communes are the same – some share everything including their money, but others allow each separate 'unit' as much privacy as they feel they need, provided the general health and happiness of the community do not suffer.

Our knowledge of community living, gained from a group in Suffolk, revealed that though some of the adults had grumbles and grievances, the general atmosphere was one of serenity and contentment. But for the children it was paradise. The idea of babysitting never arose – there were always sufficient people around to keep an eye open. The children knew and trusted all the grown-ups and would go to any of them for help if necessary. None of the irritations and jealousies that so often threaten the small enclosed family seemed to be in evidence. For the children of one-parent families there were plenty of extra mums and dads around, and for only children there were lots of brothers and sisters. It seemed to us that communal living had a lot to recommend it, especially for those with young families. To find out more about communes or communities, contact the Alternative Communities Movement (see Directory).

Reorganize Your Working Life

If shared living is not the sort of solution you're looking for, perhaps your best plan would be to reorganize the pattern of your working life. Thousands of men and women have changed their lifestyles so that they can look after their children themselves. It *can* be done. The most obvious way is for *either* parent to be a home-based freelance worker; many jobs can be done in this way. Artists, craftsmen, journalists, accountants, private teachers and tutors, dressmakers, landladies, architects, information scientists, typists, telephone salespeople, cooks and caterers, childminders and playgroup leaders, photographers or home computer workers (a blossoming new world) – these are just a few of the people who can work from home for the most part.

Many women and somewhat fewer men switch their type or method of working once their child is born so that they can be both full-time worker and full-time parent. Many still need extra paid help to survive, but they may be able to manage with straightforward domestic help rather than child care.

It is also possible for either or both parents to work part-time, which means that either or both can usually be at home for the children. In 1980 four-and-a-half million people in the UK worked part-time. Some employers allow their workers to share one job between them, and this paired-work system can open up further alternatives. We've come across paired teachers, laundrette supervisors, bank cashiers and shop assistants, and there must be many more. If they carry the pairing idea to its logical conclusion and pair the child care, too, one could look after two sets of children while the other is out at work. The paired workers can, of course, be a husband-and-wife team. For instance, two friends of ours are taxi-drivers, sharing a cab. As a rule Ann drives it during the day while Bill does the shopping and housework. Bill takes over in the late afternoon so that Ann can be at home with the children and cook the evening meal. Bill gets home very late, Ann leaves home very early, and they both work very hard. Occasionally they take a day off together and the whole family piles into the cab and goes to the sea-side. The treat is all the more fun because it is so rare for all of them to be together.

Jobs which offer 'flexi-time' arrangements – as so many local government posts do nowadays – can *ease* the need for child care since they enable parents to choose the hours they work to fit in with their children's hours at school. But they aren't a complete answer for the parent with pre-school children because they do require the same number of hours as any full-time job and during some of these hours the worker will almost certainly have to find someone else to look after the children.

Obviously it can be a great help if a parent is able to take a child to work, and good workplace nurseries are an ideal solution. But even if there is no nursery, you *may* be able to take your child to work with you. Young babies in particular can be quite easy to cope with while still in the pram and carry-cot stage, and the newspapers abound with stories of working women including top executives, politicians, writers, TV programme presenters, actresses, singers and so on, who insist on baby going, too. At the other end of the income scale many cleaning ladies take their own child to work with them. The point is that cleaning ladies and successful media workers have this in common, amongst other things – they are in demand and therefore their employers are prepared to put up with the baby in order to keep the mother.

And sometimes it is perfectly easy. A woman running or assisting in a small shop, or with her own office, can probably look after the baby and work at the same time just as effectively as if she were self-employed and running a business from home. Many people have been successful at this. So if you feel you are really needed and valued and *if* the conditions in which you work would make it possible to accommodate a carry-cot, necessary toys and so on, and *if* your baby is reasonably well-behaved and isn't likely to cry all day, have a go. Put the suggestion to your boss and see what the reaction is. There may be a useful spin-off to this – s/he may be so horrified at the thought of a baby distracting the entire office staff that s/he'll feel there's no way out but to establish a nursery! Feel your way carefully before you put the idea forward, and don't be too aggressive, make threats, or try to lay down conditions. Be prepared for opposition and meet it with reasoned persuasion.

Reorganize Your Social Life

Perhaps the time is ripe to use the same positive thinking about your babysitting arrangements during leisure time as has been suggested for work. Many parents are accustomed to taking tiny babies with them in carry-cots when they go out to supper, a party, or to visit friends or family. In fact, older children can be taken along, too. Only in Britain do we have this rigid idea that children ought to be in their own beds by a certain time. In many continental countries, for example, children tend to stay up much later and share the evening with their parents. While it is not really going to help you to enjoy your party more to have your children joining in the fun with gusto, it may well be possible to take them along with you, let them say 'hello', and then firmly tuck them up in a spare bed. They'll hardly wake when you carry them home a few hours later, and you'll *all* have had a good evening without the worry or expense of babysitters.

It is worth persevering with this even if your child plays up a bit the first couple of times. The chances are she is just testing you out and will adapt herself once she realizes you mean business.

It is also a good idea to experiment with new ways of having an evening's entertainment. For instance, instead of going out to a pub with friends, friends could congregate in your home and bring a bottle. Instead of going out to eat in a restaurant you could invite friends to your house, each couple contributing one course or one dish and then sharing in the washing up, so that you aren't left with all the work or expense. Home-based, do-it-yourself entertainment is becoming more and more popular these days as the cost of living rises. Properly organized it can be more enjoyable than going out, and it can also solve the problem and expense of the babysitter.

It is also possible to involve children in your hobbies by enrolling them in a junior section attached to your chess club, dramatic society, disco night or whatever. An interesting article printed recently in a women's magazine showed how this could be arranged: 'Nobody needs a babysitter in Ellesmere Variety Group. They bring their children along to join in. While the adults practise their singing with the producer the little ones learn to dance with her daughter.' You could easily adapt this idea to your own interests and needs. Or *you* could take an interest in your *child*'s hobbies – learning a sport like tennis or how to play a musical instrument may put you on par and add to your relationship.

A couple could also consider separating for the occasional evening, one going out while the other stays at home with the children. There is no reason at all why each should not develop his or her own individual social life to some extent. Often separate interests strengthen a relationship. However, if you feel that this gives rise to jealousies or temptations, perhaps you should drop the idea. The expense of a babysitter is trivial compared with the pain of a broken marriage.

The fact is that there are all sorts of ways in which you can organize both your working and your family life to *minimize* your dependence on babysitters and child-care systems. But it's unlikely that you'll be able to do without them altogether. Parents need time off from their children just as much as children need a break from their parents. So search for your sitters carefully, treat them with kind consideration, and they'll almost certainly make life more livable for all of you.

8
SIMPLE STEPS TO SELF-HELP

The Babysitting Circle

The Swap System

This can be the most rewarding and easiest self-help system of all. One of the best swaps is a whole-night swap. When you want an evening out, or just some peace, your child spends the whole night at a friend's place, and another time your friends leave their child at yours. You may think you have no friends who would be interested in a scheme of this sort, but your *child* may have such a friend, and it is they, not the parents, who need to get on well.

Obviously, you need to meet the other parents and see if they are suitable for your child, but once you know them the first step could simply be to ask them if their child would like to spend a night in your home. Then just wait and see if the favour is returned!

First though, make sure that they are likely to take care of your child properly. For example, it could be very distressing for her to experience a different punishment system. If it works, it can be great fun for everyone. One of the best moments can be waking up in the morning and realizing you don't have to cope with a child – an experience which can also make you freshly aware of how much you enjoy her.

Speak to the child about it beforehand as you would for an adventure or special treat. But don't talk about it too much or she may become apprehensive. Make sure that first time you are at home and within reach, just in case she's unhappy and needs to be back in your arms. And don't forget to take along that special toy or comforter without which sleep is impossible. Keep an eye open to see how the children manage together: they will feel rejected if they think they are being forced. They must *want* to spend the night together.

Swaps can obviously be arranged for shorter or longer times.

You could swap a whole weekend for three long evenings to fit in with the needs of both sets of parents.

The Token System

This doesn't involve any money and is extremely easy to organize. A group of couples are given a dozen tokens each – cards, beans or curtain rings will do nicely – as well as a list of the telephone numbers of everyone in the group. This can have any number of members from two to fifty, but the ideal is probably about a dozen. When one couple wants an evening out they phone round. One of the other mothers or fathers comes to sit and receives one token per hour. That parent then has lots of tokens with which s/he can pay sitters. Before one couple can get more than their fair share of evenings out they run out of tokens and need to sit for others in order to build up their number again. Each parent or couple makes its own arrangements, usually sticking to two or three people on the list but with the rest of the group to fall back on if needed.

To start such a group going, all you have to do is to drop a note explaining the system to a few parents in your area and ask them to an informal meeting in your home. An advertisement in a shop window might be a good beginning if you can't think of anyone to approach personally. The actual meeting tends to run itself, as everybody wants to be helpful in order to get some help back!

A good rule is to insist that two tokens are paid for each hour after midnight and that, while two hours and five minutes should only cost two tokens, two and a quarter hours should cost three. Generosity is usually returned. It is probably *not* a good idea to combine tokens with cash – for example, paying three tokens plus £2 for a five-hour sit. This means that one couple gets extra evenings out while the other only makes a little money, and that is not the object of the exercise.

The Book System

This can start with just a few parents sitting for each other and easily grows. 'The Book' is simply a collection of all the names, addresses and telephone numbers of people who are willing to babysit for each other when available. One person keeps the book for a month at a time, and anyone wanting a sitter contacts the book-keeper to get a list of two or three possible names. When the month is up another member keeps the book. A single source of referrals means no individual is asked constantly while others are not contacted at all. The system is working well in Hull with a circle of twenty-five members who only need to keep the book about once in every two years, and the rewards greatly outweigh that minor commitment.

Skill-Swapping

Instead of babysitting for each other, you could swap skills or do a particular chore in return for babysitting or child care. If you own a car, you could take a neighbour shopping or her children to school every morning in return for an evening's free babysitting each week. Or you may be able to make or alter clothes, cook special meals, *enjoy* ironing, type or perform useful legal or accountancy chores. Any of these skills could be swapped for a spell of babysitting once you have both assessed, to your mutual satisfaction, their comparative value. Perhaps it's easiest just to work it out hour for hour – three hours of babysitting to be swapped for three hours of knitting, carpentry, washing, gardening or whatever.

Set Up An Agency

If you find it difficult to recruit people for any sort of babysitting self-help, consider helping yourself by starting a babysitting agency of your own and approaching the problem in a business-like way. The idea has much to commend it.

★ You will never be short of babysitters yourself when you need them.

★ You will be providing a useful and needed service.

★ You might make a little money.

A letter to your local paper appealing for sitters may be all you'll need to get started. Once you've interviewed and selected your work force you'll have to advertise. Again, use the local paper as well as postcard advertisements in local shops. And then you'll have to spend a little time by your telephone – unless you can afford an answering machine – to take the queries and bookings as they come in. If you provide a good, reliable, reasonably-priced service right from the beginning, you probably won't need to go on advertising for very long. Your reputation will spread like wildfire among parents in your area.

Don't attempt to go too far afield. Fares can add enormously to the price that has to be charged, and travel can add to the organizational complications. You won't make a fortune out of this sort of business – nobody does – but you will appreciate the work and involvement if you need or want it (and it will solve your own babysitting problem).

The sitters should all charge the same hourly fee and be expected to pay back a proportion of their money to you. Sometimes this is a percentage – about 15% is fair – or it can be their earnings for the first hour. An agency often works to the benefit of a sitter who is trying to earn a fair amount of money, since it can provide her with a lot of regular work and keep her constantly employed. You should point this out when you first enlist sitters and make a clear contract with them to abide by the rules, for your mutual benefit.

Keep careful records of your sitters and your customers. Just as you will have to drop bad sitters who prove to be unreliable, irresponsible or dishonest, so you'll have to keep a blacklist of customers. They may refuse to pay the sitter a proper fee or abuse her in other ways, making themselves more of a nuisance than they are worth. Fortunately, most sitters and parents will approach you in good faith and give you no trouble. However, it is wise to play safe right from the beginning – ask for references from all concerned, *and* follow them up.

Remember that the service you are offering is based on good babysitters who provide satisfactory care as well as your ability to supply them on demand. Imagine yourself in the position of the parents (which shouldn't be too difficult) if you ever need reminding.

Be A Childminder

Another way of helping yourself in a business-like way is to become a childminder, looking after two or three other children as well as your own and earning money in the process.

If you want to be a childminder your first step should be to go along to the social services department and tell them. Ask if there are any suitable training courses you could take part in as preparation. They will certainly want to be sure that your house is safe, that there is no fire risk, that you have sufficient room for children to play, and that your lavatory, bathroom and kitchen are adequate. They will also want to ascertain that you are healthy and of good character. If they are satisfied they will put your name on their list, and you will also be free to advertise personally. They will probably visit you from time to time, and they may help you by telling you how to borrow first-aid kits and safety equipment and putting you in touch with the local toy library, if there is one.

However, depending upon where you live, their support and interest may be half-hearted, so you should make some effort to help yourself. The best way to do this is by becoming a member of the National Childminding Association (see Directory). You will have to pay a small fee to join, but in return you will receive a newsletter four times a year telling you what's going on in the childminding world; you may be able to join one of their local childminders' groups – if there isn't one in your area, perhaps you could start one yourself; and they will offer you all sorts of help and advice – sending you leaflets, recommending books, and telling you about training courses.

In fact, it's probably a good idea to get in touch with the association *before* you decide whether or not you'd like to be a minder. It's not a particularly easy job, nor is it well paid or protected. On the other hand, the work is vitally important – the quality of care children receive during their early years has a powerful effect on the way they grow up and their eventual success and happiness as adults. Make sure that you really do like other people's children well enough to have them around all day, perhaps from 8 am to 6 pm or even longer. Remember that they won't always be good and charming. Sometimes they'll be dirty, naughty and irritating, cross and quarrelsome. But *you* will always have to be kind and patient. That's difficult enough with children of your own, but with other people's children it can be almost impossible. And you won't just have to look after them and keep them safe and clean. You should be prepared to entertain and play with them, read to them, tell them stories and talk to them, take them out for walks to parks and playgrounds, feed them, and take them to the baby clinic and/or playgroup if their parents wish. It really is quite an undertaking, so make sure you understand what you are letting yourself in for first and that you're sufficiently interested in children and the way they develop to do the job properly.

The self-help schemes outlined above are very simple to organize. There are others, like the next ones we'll discuss, which may seem much more difficult. But no-one should be put off by their apparent complication, for they are not as daunting as they may at first appear. Once you have understood the simple steps which lead towards a successful conclusion, the rest is child's play!

Run A Playgroup

For instance, if there isn't a playgroup in your community and you think that there should be (and you wouldn't mind organizing it), there are several steps you can take towards getting one established. But first, before you do anything else at all, write to the Pre-school Playgroups Association (see Directory), telling them what you have in mind and asking for any advice and helpful literature they can send you.

Step One – Do Your Homework

Try to find out whether there really is a need for a playgroup. Talk to other mothers of young children in your neighbourhood and see how many say very firmly, 'Yes, if there were a playgroup I'd send my child'. A group can function quite happily with as few as half a dozen.

Step Two – Consider The Premises

Decide where it will be held. If you are thinking of using your own house you'll need to ask the social services department whether it is suitable. They'll be particularly interested in safety, fire risk, and adequate space and toilet facilities. If you are thinking of renting a hall the same sort of checks will have to be made, and you'll have the added problem of finding enough money to pay the rent and provide heating and lighting. You may also have the worry of getting on well with the caretaker, who may not welcome the thought of a group of noisy children tumbling about everywhere.

Step Three – Consider The Finances

Think carefully about money. Work out how many children you will need to enroll to pay your way, and how much you will have to charge. You will *need* money for some, or all, of the things on this list – and perhaps a few more:

* rent
* heat (this is very expensive for halls and necessary for children for at least eight or nine months of the year)
* light
* insurance
* play equipment (crayons, paint and brushes, paper, books, games and toys)
* salaries (you should try to employ at least one experienced person)
* stationery and postage
* first-aid kit (disinfectant, antiseptic ointment, elastoplast, bandages, dressings, junior aspirin, and calamine lotion)
* cleaning materials

You may *receive* money from some or all of these sources:

* fees from parents
* fund-raising activities
* donations
* grants

Budgeting is very important, so do take pains to get it right. Work out all your costs as accurately as possible: don't be ludicrously optimistic, and do take inflation into account. The simplest way is to work out what *each session* of about two hours will cost for each separate item, and then to multiply the number of sessions in order to work out weekly, monthly, and annual costs. Once you have worked out a realistic budget, don't overspend. If you suddenly find yourself facing an unexpected expense, your best plan is to organize an extra money-raising activity especially to pay the bill rather than put your basic pattern of expenditure totally out of balance.

And don't think you can skimp on insurance. You must have *Public Liability Insurance* which will cover you if any accident happens to children, parents, helpers or members of the public for which you could be held liable. Make sure that it will apply both inside the building and on group outings. If you have paid staff you will also have to have *Employers' Liability Insurance*, and you can take out *Personal Accident Insurance* which will pay compensation in the case of accidents which were no-one's fault. The premises you use for your playgroup may already be insured – if so, get this confirmed in writing before you begin. Finally, if your treasurer has to take care of funds that she can't always get into the bank at the end of the day, it might be wise to have them insured against theft. If you're lucky your local authority or community council may run a comprehensive insurance scheme in which local voluntary groups can take part. If so, it will make the whole business easier and probably cheaper, too, so don't miss out on this.

Step Four – Fulfil The Requirements

You will need to apply to the social services department for registration. If the playgroup is to be in your house, *you* will be registered as a *childminder*. If it's to be held in a hall, *it* will be registered as a *day nursery*. In your letter of application you should state:

★ how many children you hope to have in the group – including any of your own

★ how many sessions you hope to hold each week

You must also apply to the local planning committee for 'change of use' permission if no playgroup has been held on the premises before, and to the fire department for inspection and approval. These three consents:

★ registration

★ planning permission, and

★ fire precaution

must be received *in writing* before you start. And you should be prepared for the fact that they may take *several* months.

Step Five – Get to Grips With The Groundwork

During this time you could get your group of interested

parents together for a series of meetings in which you would discuss in detail:

★ how the playgroup will be staffed, run and managed

★ how many parents will be needed to help, and how often

★ what equipment should be acquired, and how (some may be donated or specially made by helpful parents and well-wishers; other things will have to be bought, either new or second-hand, or hired)

★ what activities will be organized for the children, either indoors or out, in hot weather or cold

★ how the money will be raised, spent, and organized

Step Six – Organize Fund-Raising Activities

This includes both self-help money-raising events *and* applying for grants from various bodies. All sorts of books are available which will give you good advice about the best ways of raising money. For instance, the Directory of Social Change publishes *Raising Money from Trusts, Raising Money from Government, Raising Money from Industry* and *Raising Money through Special Events*, all of which can be obtained by writing direct to them (see Directory). The National Association of Youth Clubs has put out a useful publication called *Money Raising A-Z*, and Fair Play for Children produces a fact sheet, *How to Raise Funds*. A comprehensive handbook by Hilary Blume, titled *Fund Raising*, is published by Routledge and Kegan Paul (see Directory and Booklist).

Basically, fund-raising requires energy, enthusiasm and determination. It also needs good, sound organization, probably by a small committee or fund-raising officer and lots and lots of helpers. If the project for which you're raising funds is well known and respected, money will come in more easily. Fortunately, most people approve of any organization aimed at making children's lives happier – though not necessarily of making their parents' lives easier – so your playgroup should meet with generous support if you work hard at public relations and meeting people.

The Pre-school Playgroups Association has a lot of experience in applying for grants and will advise you how to take your first steps. They publish their own useful booklet, called *Grants and How to Apply for Them* (see Directory). You will have more chance of getting local authority funds for your playgroup if it has been set up according to the PPA's model constitution than if you're a private group, trying to go it alone.

Step Seven – Make Contacts

Quite apart from children, staff and parents, playgroups need supporters, advisers, backers and a body of goodwill. At this period, while you're waiting to get going, you should be making contact with all sorts of helpful people from magistrates to local councillors who could be of use to you if you run into difficulties.

During the waiting period you should also be running through a checklist to make sure that, when those three vital permissions come through at last, you've thought of everything and are really ready to go. Your playgroup checklist should cover:

★ play equipment (see that you've got enough and that it's sturdy and safe)

★ storage (you must have room to stash away all your equipment between sessions)

★ coats (you must have some form of low hooks and coathangers so that the children can cope on their own – remind parents to label clothes and name shoes)

★ lavatories (make sure that you have portable steps or boxes, if necessary, so that the children can reach them)

★ towels (personally-owned towels are safer and prevent the spread of infection. Either remind parents to supply named hand-towels or provide paper ones.)

★ first aid (the playgroup will need a first-aid kit, and those who are going to help in any capacity should have a basic knowledge of how to use it. Now could be the time for them to go to first-aid classes, or get a good illustrated handbook and do some homework. The British Red Cross – see Directory – and St John's Ambulance Brigade put on short courses in most areas. You should also have an accident book which should record every accident, with details of how, when and where it happened, exactly what happened, and what action was taken.)

★ register (you must have a list of all the children's names, along with their ages, addresses and telephone numbers, *plus* the address and phone number of the place where their parents can be reached during the playgroup session, *plus* the name and phone number of their family doctors. You should also keep a waiting list for those not able to get into the playgroup when it first opens.)

Once the great day comes, permissions are granted, staff engaged, volunteers enlisted from among parents, and the first children tumble through the doors, you will probably find that the playgroup runs quite smoothly. But you should never think you have solved all problems and know all the answers. Try to find sufficient time to keep on asking questions, keep on learning, and keep in touch with all the new developments in education-through-play. By going to courses and lectures, reading, listening to other people's experience and discussing your own, you can give your playgroup the chance to grow, and to enrich successive generations of mothers and children.

The steps outlined above, here applied to setting up a playgroup, can be used as a guide for any form of self-help child-care scheme you might like to set up. For instance, if you don't want to be committed all year round but feel that you have sufficient time and energy for a short sharp burst, it might be a good idea to consider running a holiday playscheme.

Running a School-Based Holiday Playscheme

That splendid organization Fair Play for Children (see Directory) presents a powerful lobby to persuade local education authorities to allow the community to use schools and their grounds during holidays, and they will help you considerably if you decide to go ahead with such a play project.

Step One – Do Your Homework

First of all, get together two or three helpers to form a steering committee. You will have to decide:
★ how many children you expect to cater for, what their ages will be, when the playscheme will function and for how many hours a day;

★ where the money will come from for staff, insurance, equipment, administration and secretarial costs, and approximately how much you will need;

★ what activities you will organize – sports, outings, arts and crafts, etc;

★ how many paid and voluntary workers you will need, and where you will find them;

★ whether you need any special facilities – lavatories, cloakrooms, kitchens and so on.

Step Two – Consider The Premises

When you know exactly what your proposals are, start investigating the area and applying to the school of your choice. Do this well ahead, as the wheels of bureaucracy take a long time a-turning! When choosing which schools to put on your shortlist, think about the practicalities. Are they conveniently situated and easy to get to by unescorted children or parents without cars? Are they open-plan, or divided up into smaller classrooms which are usually easier to cope with? Do they have good facilities, like tennis courts, sports fields, swimming pools, and so on? Are their caretakers friendly (very often a play project stands or falls purely on the organizer's relationship with the caretaker, so this is very important and worth working at)?

Once you have decided which school would be most suitable, write to the Chief Education Officer. You can get the address from the library if you can't find it in the telephone book. Find out whether there is an agreed policy on community use of schools and whether there is a special clause recommending community use in the Rules of Management for School Governors. You should also check whether the education authority runs its own insurance scheme to cover community use or whether you must get your own insurance cover.

Next write to the head teacher of the school of your choice, outlining briefly what you want to do, and ask for an appointment so that you can discuss your proposals. Her or his response may well depend upon how responsible, well-prepared and organized you seem to be and whether you can inspire confidence in your ability to cope. The head teacher's main concerns will probably be:

★ how the caretaker will react, and

★ whether there will be any damage to the school itself or to its equipment. Obviously you will explain that everything will be thoroughly insured, but that's not enough. You must show that you have made provision for proper control and supervision so that any damage will be minimal.

If, after your interview, the head teacher seems unwilling to cooperate with your scheme, it may not be worth pressing on with that school. S/he may have a perfectly valid reason for refusing you. Perhaps the school is going to be redecorated or renovated. But even if the reason seems weak, it's hardly worth having a major confrontation and gaining a lot of bad publicity in the process. It's much more sensible to go on to the next school on your list and start again.

When you do find a cooperative head teacher, you can then apply formally to the education authority for permission to go ahead with your holiday scheme. If permission is granted, congratulations. But in fact, the work is just beginning.

Step Three – Consider The Finances

Your research will have told you where the money is to come from. Now is the time to start getting it in. Until permission was granted your plans had to be tentative, but now you must confirm to the authority and other funding bodies that you will be applying for grants.

Getting a grant has already been covered in the playgroup section, but there may be other funds available for playschemes. For instance, Urban Aid is helpful in some areas – ask your local authority about it well in advance. Applications must be given priority by the council, and usually have to be submitted by February at the latest. If your work will include art, drama and music, try making application to the Arts Council (see Directory) or your own regional arts association – you may be lucky. The *Directory of Grant-making Trusts* (see Directory), an expensive but useful book, can be consulted in the reference department of your local library.

If you decide to set up as a charity – you could ask a friendly lawyer to help you to do this, or ask your local Council of Voluntary Service for advice – you will find there are many advantages, for this or any other scheme. To start with, many trusts won't even consider an application from anyone who isn't a registered charity. Secondly, charities are exempt from income tax, corporation tax, and capital gains tax. They can get a 50% reduction of rates on their premises – more at the discretion of the local authorities.

To register as a charity you must draw up a constitution which clearly lays down the aims and objects of your project, and this must be formally adopted at a public meeting which has been advertised in the local press. Then the minutes of this meeting, plus the constitution, must be sent to the Charity Commissioners for approval and registration.

You must organize your insurance, too, and as well as those required for a playgroup you may need to consider vehicle insurance. If play-leaders or volunteers are using or lending their own cars to transport children, the insurance company should be notified. If you borrow a van, take care: it may only be registered for goods, not passengers. If so, you will either need to alter the provision or find another means of transport. *Don't* take the risk and trust that nothing will happen. It *might*.

Step Four – Fulfil The Requirements

Before you make any detailed plans for holiday activities you need to know exactly what is allowed, which of the school facilities you can use, and for how long. And then you need to make sure that the workers and children involved know what is permitted and what is not, and that they will stick to it. You should also find out about things that may seem trivial but can make all the difference the *next* time you apply to use the school. For instance, do you provide the first-aid kit, or can you use the school's; are you supposed to clean the loos and kitchens, or is that a service included in the deal – and if so, will you have to pay extra for it?

Step Five – Get To Grips With The Groundwork

Next you need to work out some sort of programme of activities. Ensure that you have sufficient helpers at all times, probably working on a rota system, and that you have adequate play and sports equipment. You also need to make sure, perhaps by means of a duplicated information sheet, that everyone knows exactly who is doing what, when and where.

When the playscheme is all over bar the shouting, it's still not *quite* over as far as the organizers are concerned. Do:

★ leave the school immaculate – even if it wasn't immaculate when you arrived;

★ thank the school staff for their help – perhaps a little appreciation gift for the caretaker;

★ thank the Education Officer for his or her help and provide some information about how the scheme worked out. If it has been a notable success it may encourage more cooperation next time a similar request is received;

★ ask the local paper to carry a story, with photographs, about your project.

Good publicity of this sort is invaluable for other years and other groups. It all adds up to confirming the basic philosophy that schools are for sharing and using, the whole year round.

If permission for your holiday scheme is refused – commiserations. But don't give up. First of all, try to find out why it has been refused, and whether it should have been. It sometimes happens that though there is a clause encouraging, or at least permitting, the community use of a school in the Rules of Management, the governors have either preferred to ignore it or are genuinely unaware of it. If you can prove that this is so, you can challenge the decision. It's sometimes better to make an oblique approach through a useful contact. For instance, it's possible that someone in your group knows a member of the staff of the school in question, or one of the governors, or a councillor who is on the education committee. If so, try to get them on your side and ask them to find out what went wrong.

If the education authority is absolutely opposed to the community use of schools, give them information about successful schemes in other parts of the country – Fair Play for Children (see Directory) will help with this – and the sound economic and social reasons that show this is a very sensible idea. To be honest, it's highly unlikely that you will be able to change anyone's mind sufficiently to be able to go ahead with your playscheme during that holiday period, but perhaps the next time you ask for permission, or another group follows in your footsteps, it *will* be granted.

Splendid though a holiday playscheme may be, it is not enough in itself to be of much use to full-time working parents, who need child care throughout all the holidays as well as in the nasty tea-time gaps. However, it's possible to use one as a trial run and to develop it, once you've learnt how to cope, into a much more ambitious project. Many, many people need good latch-key care for their children, but it is rarely provided, except in one or two imaginative inner city areas. So the only speedy solution to the problem is a do-it-yourself scheme.

Organizing Out-of-School Day Care

The way to set up such a scheme should by now be familiar, for it is much the same step-by-step process as for any other self-help scheme.

First, find out who needs it. Various people may be able to help you do this. If there's a Gingerbread group in your area, they may know approximately how many single parents need day care of this sort. Another useful organization which is particularly concerned with low-income families is the Child Poverty Action Group (see Directory). The National Society for the Prevention of Cruelty to Children may know of children who are frequently left alone and unsupervised. And health visitors, social workers, organizers of day nurseries and school teachers often know which families are in need of support. Check what facilities already exist to help these people, and then work out whether there is a real gap between what is needed and what is available.

If there is, you are ready to begin. Get your supporters together by calling a meeting. This should be both well publicized and well organized. Find a hall you can use, preferably free or for a nominal fee, that is conveniently situated. (You can make a collection at the end of the meeting to pay your expenses if necessary.) Advertise it by putting up notices in public places parents are likely to use – schools, baby clinics, laundrettes, post offices, and so on. Distribute some leaflets street by street – often a paper shop will put notices into papers for a tiny charge, and this is very cost-effective. And ask your local paper to carry a little chat piece about your scheme – battling parents are always good copy. Find a chair person for the meeting, provide her with a list of topics to be discussed, and make sure that she organizes things well enough to come up with a list of conclusions before the meeting ends. She should also try to get a list of all those people who volunteered to help in any way at all and those who are willing to join a working party to get on with the next phase of the operation.

After the meeting, it's a good idea to send everyone who turned up an account of what actually happened, an indication of what's going to happen next, a list of names and addresses of those who volunteered to help, and a request for more people to help, especially in areas which haven't yet been covered. You really need to enlist the services of someone who can use a typewriter and has access to a duplicator or cheap copier, because you'll find that a lot of information has to be pushed around from person to person once the work is thoroughly underway.

The working party must now get down to the nitty-gritty of deciding what must be done when, how, and by whom – and then make a start on it. Try to work out a timetable giving yourself at least a six-month countdown to take-off. And be prepared for the fact that actually getting any money out of a government body will probably take *longer* than six months.

This period of waiting can be useful for building up contacts, friendships and informal self-help between the parents of the children who will join in the scheme. Many of them won't be able to help on a day-to-day basis, but they may be able to get involved with each other in other ways such as occasional babysitting, swapping skills, or even simple companionship. These links between parents can often be an unexpected but enormously valuable spin-off from a self-help child-care scheme, and they should be encouraged.

At last, when it has all come together – the premises, the workers, the children, the equipment, the money *and* the permissions – you are ready to start. You'll be relieved to find that actually running the out-of-school scheme is, in a way, less of a headache than getting it set up in the first place, mainly because the problems you will face are mainly practical ones rather than a frustrating battle against bureaucracy.

The first week or so may be tricky while you are all finding your feet. The children will probably be a little apprehensive, wondering what is expected of them and worried in case it's going to be just like school all over again. Until they feel secure they'll probably be silly and naughty. It won't be easy for the workers either, especially the volunteers who will perhaps be inexperienced. They'll be finding out whether they can manage, whether the children will accept and like them, whether they will respond to their ideas and suggestions willingly. But soon things will settle down and the scheme will be carried along by its own momentum.

Obviously the helpers will get on better if they like and understand children and positively enjoy being with them. If you find that some are there out of a sense of duty or because they are trying to test themselves in some way, watch them carefully. They may do more harm than good. If so, it should be pointed out, without acrimony, that perhaps child care isn't for them and they'd be happier doing something else. Bullies – people who can only control children by resorting to shouting and smacking – shouldn't be tolerated either.

There should be a few basic rules, mainly designed to make sure the group itself doesn't suffer through the bad behaviour of an individual, and these rules should be observed. Otherwise there is no need for rigid discipline or a complicated system of crime and punishment. Usually children who are kept happy, busy and interested are reasonably well behaved, especially if the adults in charge are capable of creating the right mood. Of course, there *are* children who are trouble-makers and who get their kicks out of spoiling the fun for everyone else, and if there's no changing them they will probably have to be excluded, but in our experience these are few and far between.

For help in setting up and running this type of project you could not do better than to read the excellent booklet *Out of School*, written by Sonia Jackson and published by the Bristol

Association for Neighbourhood Daycare (BAND) (see Directory).

Organizing Comprehensive Daycare

The easiest kind of self-help child care to organize is undoubtedly the various types of babysitting circles people work out for themselves. By far the most ambitious is a complete day-care scheme functioning daily the whole year round. This may seem beyond the reach of a voluntary group, but it *can* be done, as Gingerbread has proved with its successful Keighley Kiddicare project, founded in 1975. The scheme combines nursery care for the under-fives with before- and after-school care *and* school-holiday care for the over-fives, and it manages to do all this on a relatively low budget. The Kiddicare scheme, for thirty children but excluding holiday care, cost £16,000 per year to run in 1979. It was estimated then that it would cost the local authority about £40,000 to provide a similar scheme – and the financial gap will have widened even further now.

Kiddicare is a valuable example of what is possible. It can be used as a pilot scheme, showing other voluntary groups how to set about a somewhat daunting task: what to do and – perhaps more important – what not to do. When the Keighley Gingerbread group took over a nursery that was about to be closed, they first appointed a management committee, and it laid down the following list of prime jobs:

★ achieving charitable status so that they could raise money more easily;

★ making a plan for raising money locally;

★ working out a clear formula for the practical, day-to-day running of the nursery;

★ registering thirty children;

★ increasing cooperation with the local authority;

★ understanding clearly the needs of the children and staff, and the management committee's responsibility towards them;

★ negotiating a good lease for the premises.

It is interesting that the two at the top of the list concern money raising, which is absolutely crucial to practically any form of self-help child care. In fact, it is impossible to make a good scheme financially self-supporting without placing it beyond the means of many of those parents who most need it. In 1977 it was estimated that to make Kiddicare economically viable the fees would have to be £14 a week. Actually, they were set at between £2.50 and £8, according to what parents could afford, with the result that there was an annual deficit of £5-6,000. The lesson to be learnt is that fund raising and the attracting of grants is always a vital ingredient of the work to be done.

Significantly, one of Kiddicare's earliest financial set-backs was caused by bad advice rather than their own lack of efficiency or industry. In 1977 they applied for an Urban Aid grant, with the backing of the social services department, and were turned down. When the secretary made enquiries as to *why* the application had been unsuccessful, she discovered that most of the councillors on the planning panel had little or no knowledge of Kiddicare or its work. She found this particularly galling in that she had originally suggested to the social services department that she approach *all* Keighley councillors and tell them about Kiddicare's work, but she had been advised against this on the grounds that it would seem too much like pressuring. She had taken their advice. It was an expensive mistake, costing £25,000. Fortunately, this sad story had a happy ending. A second approach was made to Urban Aid in the following year, but not until all the councillors had been told about Kiddicare and the value of its work. This time, the application was successful. This is a valuable lesson to be learnt. When public funds are being sought, effective lobbying of those who hold the purse strings is a must. To find out more about setting up a comprehensive scheme like Kiddicare, read *Self-Help Day Care Schemes*, a useful, factual and practical booklet written by Julie Kaufman and available from Gingerbread (see Directory).

We have reached some absolutely basic conclusions in our research into self-help child care of all types. The successful ones owe their success, to a large extent, to:
★ careful, detailed planning and organization both before the

scheme begins and once it is in operation;

★ good publicity and pleasant relationships with the community;

★ effective fund raising for the more ambitious ones.

If you can master these, then whatever project you undertake should thrive. But do remember, amidst all the work and organization, that looking after children should be fun, not a dreary chore. Laughter, happiness, play, love and learning – *that* is what it's all about.

APPENDIX

BE YOUR OWN GINGER GROUP

If you find after reading this book that the child care available to you does not meet your needs in terms of its amount, quality or cost, and that self-help child-care schemes do not provide the answer, you may decide to try persuading your local government or employers to do more. And persuasion – or pressure or lobbying, whatever it's called – is not necessarily difficult. It can be as simple as writing a letter to the parish council asking for permission to use one of their recreation grounds as the base for a holiday playscheme. On the other hand, it can be a nationwide project involving the lobbying of MPs, huge demonstrations and massive media coverage.

In this appendix we have set out two patterns for possible campaigns, one to persuade the local authority to provide better child-care facilities for the under-fives, the other to persuade your employer to set up a workplace nursery. They may seem slightly formidable to those who aren't used to community action, but, of course, many others simpler to organize could be handled using the same approach.

Widening the Campaign For Better Local Authority Child-Care Provision

If you want to set up a ginger group to pressure your local authority, the first thing you need to know is that it will be hard work, demanding time and organization. Secondly, it will take a certain amount of money. Some will be needed just to pay for stamps, notepaper and telephone calls, and if you are to expand into posters, leaflets and advertisements, and perhaps even hold public meetings, it will cost much more.

You can get your group together by:
★ persuading people you know, who are in similar difficulties, to support you; and
★ advertising in the local authority area.

If you are a young mother with small children you probably know others. They may be personal friends or people you meet at the baby clinic, mother-and-toddler club or wherever. If you are a single parent you may come across them at the local Gingerbread group or Singles Club. You will probably have a good idea of whether they have problems finding care for their children and whether they are likely to support you in a battle with the local authority. So start by inviting some of them round to your place, put your ideas to them, and ask for their help. If you feel that the numbers are disappointing, hire a hall for an evening, put an advertisement in the local paper and invite anyone interested to come along.

Make sure that you have a good, strong chairperson for the meeting, and work out very carefully beforehand what message you want to put over, what exactly you want to achieve, and what sort of methods you can use to achieve it. By the time the meeting is over you should have a list of names and addresses of people who have offered help and of what sort of help they can give – typing, letter writing, poster making, fund raising, etc. – and an idea of what shape the campaign will take.

The next step will be to divide your supporters into action committees. You'll need a central committee to hold the whole thing together, and that should include:

★ a chairperson to run the meetings;
★ a secretary to keep the minutes, write the letters, and so on;
★ a treasurer to keep a check on income and expenses; and
★ two or three members to help them.

Then you'll need one or two small groups with specific duties – one to raise funds, one to do research and one to be responsible for lobbying and publicity.

Fund raising   This need not be a major worry, because the amount of money you will need won't be huge. The easiest way is probably through a couple of jumble sales, or you could hire a market stall on a few occasions. Or you could organize a fête, fair or concert – often local groups of amateur singers or actors are longing to give their services free for a cause of which they approve. Many ideas for fund-raising events are suggested in the books recommended in Chapter Eight, but whatever you choose to do, bear three points in mind:

111

★ the unreliability of good weather. Have alternative arrangements lined up and publicized.

★ making worthwhile profits. Do your sums carefully, never under-estimate your expenses or be wildly optimistic about your income, and make sure that the event will be sufficiently well-publicized and attractive to bring in a big attendance.

★ supporting a good cause. People will only come and support your events if they think your *cause* deserves support. Again, fund raising and publicity go hand in hand.

Research When asking for public funds you *must* know the relevant facts, such as how many places are already provided, or planned for, in day-care nurseries, child centres, and extended-day playgroups in your area; what, if any, latch-key facilities are available.

Your local planning department is a good source of information, as well as the education and social services department. Just go and ask – the information is not secret. If you live under a good authority like Bristol they will *want* to tell you about the various activities and facilities available. For example, the enterprising London borough of Camden publishes a booklet called *What's Where for the Under-Fives in Camden*, which covers a whole range of care from council nurseries to Young Family Care Centres, toy libraries and occasional creches (available from the town hall). If your authority has no useful organized information available, ask why not, and press for better details of what's available to be published and widely distributed. Lack of information probably means that they provide very few facilities. If that is the case, they may have money left from funds designed to be spent in this way, and should be persuaded to spend it forthwith.

The information you need falls into the following categories:

★ the number of full- and part-time registered places;
★ the hours of availability;
★ the cost to parents;
★ the size of waiting lists;
★ how priority is assessed;
★ how the local authority calculates the overall need for places in its area;

★ whether there is a local Social Services Consultative Committee for Under-Fives – and if so, what it is doing.

Having calculated the provision, you next need to ascertain approximately how much of what kind of child care is needed, and where the gaps and weaknesses are. You may need to have a questionnaire drawn up and do house-to-house investigations for this. Or you could take a sample by questioning women at baby clinics, primary schools, nursery classes, playgroups and so on, as well as those who work locally in factories, big stores and offices. If there is a Gingerbread group in your town, find out if it has any useful local statistics. Single parents are particularly in need of support, so Gingerbread may want to help with your campaign.

You should also be on the lookout for facts and figures about:
★ individual cases where lack of day care has caused a family to be split up, face the threat of having the children taken into care, or force the parent/s to lose their jobs;
★ cases where children are left untended or badly cared for because of lack of facilities;
★ cases where the hours nurseries are open make it impossible for parents to fit them in with their working day;
★ cases where high costs put nursery places beyond the reach of lower-paid parents; and
★ cases where nurseries are difficult to reach for those without cars.

Then collect examples of what other local authorities are doing to meet the need. A publication called *Under-Fives*, produced by the Association of County Councils (see Directory), lists a wide variety of good ideas and innovations that have been put into practice. You could also ask the Equal Opportunities Commission (see Directory) for advice, more examples and a reading list.

At this point work out specifically what *your group* wants from *your local authority*; formulate and present your demands to *both* the social services and the education departments. Be reasonable in your requests. Utopia won't be with us for a long time yet. For instance, it has been pointed out that extended-day playgroups cost very much less to run than day nurseries, so you could make this a useful plank in your argument. It's also worth outlining the fact that community nurseries, set up and run by community organizations with financial assistance from local authorities, provide high-quality care at comparatively low cost. If they were supported and positively encouraged by both central and local government they could go a long way towards helping bridge the shortfall between the full-time day-care places provided and those required.

A very good experimental scheme is in operation in Lambeth in South London. There the authority itself employs childminders, instead of leaving them to make a direct arrangement with each parent. It trains them and links them with a day nursery. The aim is both to improve the quality of the care they give and to improve the pay and working conditions of the minders themselves. The result of this scheme is an improvement in the service – but at a cost. In Lambeth childminding costs the council nearly as much as a place in a day nursery. Several other authorities are experimenting with courses and discussion groups for minders, and the response has been highly encouraging.

When you have completed your research and clarified your requests, combine them into a campaign document. Get it neatly typed and bound, make several copies, and send one of them to the director of social services of your local council or borough. Include a covering letter to which are added as many signatures as possible.

Lobbying Lobbying simply means arranging some time for your group to get together with local councillors or with your MP – or another MP with a known interest in promoting your cause – to try to persuade them to support your campaign.

Lobbying should be used when it seems likely that a key decision-maker might be influenced to back and promote your viewpoint among the planners and financiers who can make things happen. It gives you a chance to sit down and talk through the issue with your MP or councillors, when you can show them the strength and reasonableness of your case more effectively than a campaign document or letters alone would do.

The first thing to do is find out where and when a decision will be made and who has the power to influence it. You should find out which councillors sit on committees dealing with child-care provision. The chairperson of the committee is usually its more powerful member, so you should know who s/he is. Make enquiries at your town hall. Your local MP may be helpful because s/he can, if s/he so wishes, put pressure on the council by supporting your case. It is also useful to have contacts inside the local press.

Remember, however, that lobbying is only effective as part of your campaign if it is combined with publicity. You should, for instance, contact the local radio, press and TV company with details of your activities. Often a demonstration to support a lobby is as important as the lobby itself, because it attracts press coverage.

Councillors can be lobbied at their surgeries, their homes, at meetings, and at the town hall. Sometimes, if you ask permission to send a delegation to a meeting, the committee involved may invite you to attend and present your case – but you will only be allowed to answer questions put to you by the councillors. Take a copy of your campaign document for every member of the committee or, better still, have a copy of it given to them before the meeting so they will have time to consider it first.

MPs can be lobbied at their surgeries. You don't usually have to make an appointment, but be prepared for a long wait. Surgeries are held weekly, fortnightly or monthly and are usually advertised in the local paper – or you could ask the Citizens' Advice Bureau or ring up the local party offices. Take along all the documents with any bearing on the matter including any letters or newspaper reports that you consider important.

It is quite a good idea to contact the other parliamentary candidates in your area, too, particularly if you think they may be more sympathetic than your elected member. They may be interested in using your needs as part of *their* campaign.

You might prefer to write to your MP at the House of Commons (see Directory). Keep your letter brief, polite and to the point. Give all relevant references and addresses. Have the letter typed, if possible, and include your name, address and telephone number. And keep a copy of it for your own reference. Any other people who might be helpful should be approached in the same way.

Afterwards you must *follow up* your lobbying. If you have met people face to face, make notes as soon as possible of what was said at the meeting and then write to them immediately detailing what you understand to have been said and promised. Keep a copy of that letter and any reply you may receive. Report back to your group on the results of your meetings, letters and phone calls so that they are kept well informed, up-to-date and involved.

Publicity The first thing you need to know is whom to contact on your local papers and radio and TV stations. *Make a contact book* and enter in it all names, addresses and phone numbers of useful contacts – reporters, editors, educational correspondents and so on. Ask around until you find out who is most likely to be interested in your campaign and therefore to want to write about it.

Then *do a press release*, which describes the campaign in as bright and effective a way as possible. If it is so well put together that no editing is needed, it has more chance of being used. Make the main points in the first two paragraphs and give any extra information in a third. Keep it brief – not more than five hundred words. Type it neatly, double spaced on one side of the page only. Make sure that it has a contact name with address and telephone number so the editor can get in touch with you if s/he wishes. It's often a good idea to add a covering letter saying that you'll telephone soon to discuss the matter further – and then *do so*. Don't be frightened; reporters are pushy people themselves and they will expect others to push, too.

Local radio and television are always on the lookout for good community news and are usually hard-up financially. If you are prepared to go to their studio to be interviewed and can show that you have a lively approach to the problem, if you have done your homework properly and know exactly what you are talking about, they will probably reckon that you'd make good, cheap entertainment!

Local papers may want to cover your campaign from various angles. The fact that you are working for better child-care provision is in itself a news story, but if you can find a 'human interest' angle, too – perhaps a woman MP supporter whose own children go to a childminder – they may be more interested in doing a feature on your activities than they would have been in writing a straight news story.

A different way of using the media is to get on a phone-in programme. These are very lively, especially on local radio, and there's no reason why you shouldn't use their airspace to ask for support.

Similarly, you can write to the letters page of your local newspaper. This may attract answers, and even if they are antagonistic they will serve the purpose of keeping your campaign in the public eye, at no expense to you.

Publicity is very hard work, so do work through a publicity *group* rather than one individual to put your message across. It might be a good idea to read *Getting Across: A Publicity Guide for Voluntary Organizations*, from the National Council of Social Service (see Directory). It has much useful advice to offer.

Local authorities *are* required by law to provide a certain amount of child care for the under-fives, and they are given funds to spend on that alone. However, there is no law that says local authorities must provide care during out-of-school hours for older children. So when public money is short, even if there is such a service it will probably be one of the first to be cut. And if there isn't any provision already, it's unlikely that even the most effective ginger group will be able to persuade the council to get one going. On the other hand, a recent study by the National Consumer Council (see Directory) pointed out that two Acts of Parliament – the Children and Young Persons Act (1968) and the Education Act (1944) – made it a *duty* for local authorities to take up this responsibility, and that education departments already possess appropriate powers. One way of persuading them to face up to this duty might be to suggest that they cooperate with local industry in setting up workplace nurseries which offer facilities for school-age children as well as under-fives.

Campaign for a Workplace Nursery

The first step towards persuading an employer to provide a workplace nursery is to study what other firms have done and how successful their ventures have been. One or two examples are quoted later, but the best way to start your homework is by reading *Setting Up a Workplace Nursery*, published by and available from the Equal Opportunities Commission (see Directory).

Don't try to save time and cut corners by rushing into negotiations of this kind without doing your homework first. No employer will be impressed or persuaded by a suggestion that is not backed up by facts and figures, some understanding of the practical problems, and a clear-eyed and realistic assessment of the financial implications. For instance, it's no good saying 'I'm sure it won't cost very much' when the truth is that it will cost a great deal. It's much wiser to say, 'It will cost money but there are funds and grants available to help, *and* the running costs will be tax-deductible.'

While doing your research you should also find out in an informal way whether you would have support from your fellow-workers and whether they would use a creche, and – if you are a member of a trade union – whether your union will help you. The Trades Union Council (TUC) has a vested interest in keeping its members at work, and it may be that they are the people to conduct negotiations with your employers.

Both the National Union of Journalists and the National Association of Local Government Officers have published helpful booklets, called *Workplace Nurseries: The Why and How* and *Workplace Nurseries: A Negotiating Kit* (see Directory).

Next put your case, as well argued and presented as possible, to your employers. *Don't* be militant, aggressive or bossy. And don't make idle threats. If you say 'Give us a creche or you'll have to do without me', you will only have yourself to blame if you are unsuccessful. You could point out, in moderate terms and diplomatic phrases, that it is to their advantage to keep expensively-trained and much-needed workers who would normally be forced to leave after their children are born. You might also explain that the Employment Protection Act (1975) gives a woman the right to return to work twenty-nine weeks after the birth of her child, and that evidence shows many employers are finding this very useful in running their businesses smoothly but that it is impossible without good child-care facilities.

The fathers at your workplace may be just as keen to take advantage of a creche as the mothers and employers are not allowed by law to discriminate between men and women in providing this facility. This could enlarge your ginger group to more effective proportions.

Once the employer has given approval in principle, some formal action is necessary. A questionnaire should be issued to discover what demand there is:

★ for babies under two years old;
★ for two- to five-year-olds;
★ for school-age children after school; and
★ for holiday provision.

The results should be analyzed carefully.

Then work out whether the firm would have to provide the creche itself or if it could cooperate with other local employers and/or the local authority. If this investigation proves that a creche would be well used, there's more work to be done, and for this you'll probably need a steering committee to share the load.

Suitable premises must be found. The firm may have space in its own buildings, but on the other hand it may have to find or build extra accommodation. At this stage you should talk to the local authority planning department about any potential scheme, and take advice from the environmental health and fire departments. You should also ask the advice of the social services, education and recreation and leisure departments, because they may be able to provide you with a set of working guidelines. Much of the advice coming your way at this stage will be of a highly specialized nature.

Finally, it is important to look into finances *very* carefully. The money will probably come from three separate sources:

★ the employer(s)
★ the parents

★ outside sources
and will be needed both for *capital* costs (to set up the scheme, provide the building and equipment, and so on) and for *running* costs (to keep it operating and pay wages to helpers). If the local authority is involved – and do get them involved if you possibly can – they may be able to pay for part of the capital costs through the funds they possess for their education and social services building programmes. If the nursery is in an inner city area, special funds may be available from the Inner City Partnership Scheme.

Some employers are eligible for funding from the EEC Social Fund. Details are outlined in a booklet published by the Department of Employment called *The European Social Fund: A Guide to Possible Applicants*, available from the European Communities Commission UK Office (see Directory). And New Towns often have funds available for this sort of project if it is to be established in their area.

Charities may also help – you can find out details of these from your local council's voluntary services department. One source of help towards *staffing* might be a grant from the Manpower Services Commission, who will sometimes provide money if the project includes the training of people previously unemployed.

By this stage – and it will probably take you several months to get this far – you will have a good idea of whether the scheme is going to work. The saga of workplace nurseries is peppered with a lot of sorry failures and a few happy successes. The Royal Shakespeare Company runs a thriving creche for the children of its company and staff in Stratford. In 1980 BBC campaigners at last, after years of struggle, persuaded their management that nurseries could help further equal opportunities *and* offset recruiting and training costs by enabling them to keep their experienced workers instead of continually looking for new ones, and plans were finalized to convert part of a BBC property into a subsidized creche run by a committee representing parents, union and management. Recently in south London the combined pressure of a local nursery campaign and the Community Health Council finally won employees of the National Health Service an Urban Aid grant

120

to cover both the capital costs of a building for their proposed nursery and a substantial part of its running costs. Once again the victory was won on *economics* – they suffered a chronic shortage of trained female staff.

Special mention must be made of the Day Nursery at the Stylewear Manufacturing Company in Birkenhead, which has been running since 1966. The creche is open from 7.30 am until 5 pm and provides breakfast, lunch and tea for the children. It caters for babies of six months old up to ten-year-olds. Those at school can arrive beforehand and have breakfast there, after which they are taken to and from school by the firm's transport. At the end of the day they have tea and can play or watch television. And in the holidays they join full-time.

The results of this cooperation between employer and employees are astonishing. To start with, the return rate of women leaving to have babies is a staggering 100%. Absenteeism is only three or four per cent, although the *average* in the textile industry is twenty. And the employers' cost of subsidizing the nursery is more than offset by the benefits of retaining loyal, skilled staff. They consider it a total success. Obviously the employees do, too, for several women who were once children in the nursery are now on the staff, their own children in turn cared for by the creche!

DIRECTORY OF USEFUL ORGANIZATIONS

Alternative Communities Movement: 18 Garth Road, Bangor, North Wales.

Arts Council of Great Britain: 105 Piccadilly, London W1V 0AU.

Association of County Councils: Eaton House, 66a Eaton Square, London SW1.

Bristol Association for Neighbourhood Daycare (BAND): 9 Elmdale Road, Bristol 8.

British Association for Early Childhood Education: Montgomery Hall, Kennington Oval, London SE11 5SW.

British Association for Settlements and Social Action Centres: 7 Exton Street, London SE1 8UE.

British Red Cross Society – Services for the Handicapped: 9 Grosvenor Crescent, London SW1X 7EJ.

British Tourist Authority: 64 St James's Street, London SW1.

Central Bureau for Educational Visits and Exchanges: 43 Dorset Street, London W1.

Charities Aid Foundation: 48 Pembury Road, Tonbridge, Kent TN9 2JD.

Child Poverty Action Group: 1 Macklin Street, London WC2.

Children's House Society: 31 Tooley Street, London SE1.

Church of England Children's Society: Old Town Hall, Kennington Road, London SE11 4QD.

Colony Holidays: Linden Manor, Upper Colwall, Malvern, Worcestershire WR13 6PP.

Community Service Volunteers: 237 Pentonville Road, London N1 9NJ.

Cooperative Development Agency: 20 Albert Embankment, London SE1 5TH.

Department of Employment: 8 St James's Square, London SW1.

Directory of Social Change: 9 Mansfield Place, London NW3.

Discovery Holidays of Northern Ireland: 34 Mount Charles, Belfast BT7 1NZ.

Dr Barnardo's: Tanners Lane, Barkingside, Ilford, Essex 1G6 1QG.

Equal Opportunities Commission: Overseas House, Quay Street, Manchester M3 3HN.

European Communities Commission UK Office: 20 Kensington Palace Gardens, London W8.

Fair Play for Children: 248 Kentish Town Road, London NW5.

Federation of Personnel Services of Great Britain: 120 Baker Street, London W1M 2DE.

Gingerbread: (Head Office) 35 Wellington Street, London WC2.

(Scotland) 38 Berkeley Street, Glasgow G3.

(N. Ireland) 291 Ormeau Road, Belfast.

Handicapped Adventure Playground Association: 3 Oakley Gardens, London SW3.

Home Office: Lunar House, Wellesley Road, Croydon CR9 2BY.

House of Commons: London SW1A 0AA.

Industrial Common Ownership Movement: 8 Sussex Street, London SW1.

Inter-Action Advisory Service Ltd: 15 Wilkin Street, London NW5.

Invalid Children's Aid Association: 126 Buckingham Palace Road, London SW1W 9SB.

Joint Twinning Committee: Local Authorities Association of Great Britain, 65 Davies Street, London W1Y 2AA.

Kith and Kids: 58 The Avenue, London N10.

Lady Hoare Trust for Physically Disabled Children: 7 North Street, Midhurst, West Sussex GU29 9DJ.

London Adventure Playground Association: 16-18 Strutton Ground, London SW1 2HP.

London Nursery Campaign: c/o Surrey Docks Child Care Project, Dockland Settlement, Redriff Road, London SE16.

MIND (National Association for Mental Health): 22 Harley Street, London W1N 2ED.

National Association of Local Government Officers (NALGO): 1 Mabledon Place, London WC1.

National Association of Youth Clubs: PO Box 1, Bond Gate, Nuneaton CV11 4DB.

National Campaign for Nursery Education: 33 Hugh Street, London SW1.

National Childminding Association: 236a High Street, Bromley, Kent BR1 1PQ.

National Children's Bureau: 8 Wakley Street, London EC1V 7QE.

National Children's Home: 85 Highbury Park, London N5 1UD.

National Consumer Council: 18 Queen Anne's Gate, London SW1.

National Council of Social Service: 26 Bedford Square, London WC1B 3HU.

National Council for Voluntary Organizations: 26 Bedford Square, London WC1B 3HU.

National Educational Research and Development Trust: 32 Trumpington Street, Cambridge CB2 1QY.

National Playbus Association: 53 Beaconsfield Road, Clifton, Bristol 8.

National Playing Fields Association: 25 Ovington Square, London SW3 1LQ.

National Society for Mentally Handicapped Children: 117 Golden Lane, London EC1.

National Society for the Prevention of Cruelty to Children (NSPCC): 1 Riding House Street, London W1P 8AA.

National Union of Journalists (NUJ): 314 Gray's Inn Road, London WC1.

One-Parent Families: 225 Kentish Town Road, London NW5 2LX.

Outward Bound: 14 Oxford Street, London W1N 0HL.

PGL Young Adventure Ltd: Station Road, Ross-on-Wye, Herefordshire.

Physically Handicapped/Able-Bodied (PHAB): 42 Devonshire Street, London W1N 1LN.

Pre-school Playgroups Association: Alford House, Aveline Street, London SE11 5DH.

Robertson's Educational Travel Service: c/o Mr and Mrs J. Robertson, 44 Willoughby Road, London NW3 1RU.

Royal Association for Disability and Rehabilitation (RADAR): 25 Mortimer Street, London W1N 8AB.

Royal Society for the Prevention of Accidents (RoSPA): Common House, The Priory, Queensway, Birmingham B4 6BS.

Save the Children: Jebb House, 157 Clapham Road, London SW9 0PT.

Shaftesbury Society: Shaftesbury House, 112 Regency Street, London SW1P 4AX.

Spastics Society: 12 Park Crescent, London W1.

Toc H: Forest Close, Wendover, Buckinghamshire.

Trades Union Congress (TUC): Great Russell Street, London WC1.

Vacation Work Publications: 9 Park End Street, Oxford.

Voluntary Council for Handicapped Children: 8 Wakley Street, London EC1V 7QE.

Young Men's Christian Association (YMCA): National Centre, Lakeside, Ulverston, Cumbria LA12 8BD.

Youth Hostels Association (YHA): 14 Southampton Street, London WC2E 7HY.

BOOKLIST

Adventure Holidays (Vac-Work)

Adventure Holidays (Youth Hostels Association)

Adventure Playground by Lambert and Pearson (Penguin Books)

Care in the Home (Royal Society for the Prevention of Accidents)

Charter on Facilities for the Under-Fives (Trades Union Congress)

Children on Holiday (British Tourist Authority)

The Directory of Grant-Making Trusts (Charities Aid Foundation)

The Do-It-Yourself Nursery Campaign (London Nursery Campaign)

Educational Implications of Unsatisfactory Childminding (National Educational Research and Development Trust)

The European Social Fund: A Guide to Possible Applicants (Department of Employment)

The Facts about Accidents (Royal Society for the Prevention of Accidents)

Fund Raising by Hilary Blume (Routledge & Kegan Paul)

Getting Across: A Publicity Guide for Voluntary Organizations by C. Slader (National Council of Social Service)

Grants and How to Apply for Them (Pre-school Playgroups Association)

Handbook for Parents with a Handicapped Child by Judith Stone and Felicity Taylor (Arrow Books)

Help Starts Here (Voluntary Council for Handicapped Children)

Holiday Playscheme Kit (National Playing Fields Association)

Holiday Playschemes (National Council of Social Service)

Holidays for the Physically Handicapped (Royal Association for Disability and Rehabilitation)

How to Raise Funds (Fair Play for Children)

Keeping Accounts: A Handbook for Voluntary Organizations (National Council of Social Service)

Kith and Kids: Self-Help for Families of the Handicapped by Maurice and Doreen Collins (Souvenir Press)

Money Raising A-Z (National Association of Youth Clubs)

Not Yet Five by E. Gwenda Bartram (ESA Creative Learning)

Notes for Opportunity Groups by Dr R. E. Faulkner (Pre-school Playgroups Association)

Out of School by Sonia Jackson (Bristol Association for Neighbourhood Daycare)

Parent's Voice (National Society for Mentally Handicapped Children)

Places in Partnership (Joint Twinning Committee)

Play with a Purpose for Under-Sevens by E. M. Matterson (Penguin Books)

Play and Volunteer Directory (National Playing Fields Association)

Playgroup Publicity (Pre-school Playgroups Association)

Raising Money from Government (Directory of Social Change)

Raising Money from Industry (Directory of Social Change)

Raising Money through Special Events (Directory of Social Change)

Raising Money from Trusts (Directory of Social Change)

School Travel and Exchange (Central Bureau for Educational Visits and Exchanges)

Self-Help Day Care Schemes by Julie Kaufman (Gingerbread)

Setting Up a Workplace Nursery (Equal Opportunities Commission)

A Simple Constitution for a Holiday Playscheme (National Playing Fields Association)

Sources of Statutory Money: A Guide for Voluntary Organizations (National Council of Social Service)

Sports and Adventure Holidays (Central Bureau for Educational Visits and Exchanges)

Spotlight on Services for the Young Handicapped Child by Jessie Parfitt (National Children's Bureau)

Suggestions for Planning a Holiday Playscheme (National Playing Fields Association)

Summer Jobs in Britain (Vac-Work)

Under-Fives (Association of County Councils)

Voluntary Social Services (Bedford Square Press)

Why Lock Up Our Schools? (Fair Play for Children)

Workplace Nurseries: A Negotiating Kit (National Association of Local Government Officers)

Workplace Nurseries: The Why and How (National Union of Journalists)